Reprinted 1990; 1991; 1994

Canadian Cataloguing in Publication Data

Hoyt, Erich, 1950-
The Whales of Canada
ISBN 0-920656-31-5
1. Whales-Canada   2. Dolphins-Canada
3. Porpoises   I. Title
QL737.C4H693 1984   599.5'0971   C84-099679-9

Cover: Killer whale "spy hopping" near Robson Bight,
Vancouver Island.
Photograph by Graeme Ellis/Courtesy West Coast Whale
Research Foundation

Range maps by Roberta Voteary

Published by Camden House Publishing
(a division of Telemedia Communications Inc.)

Camden House Publishing
7 Queen Victoria Road
Camden East, Ontario K0K 1J0

Camden House Publishing
Box 766
Buffalo, New York 14240-0766

Printed and distributed under exclusive licence from
Telemedia Communications Inc. by:
Firefly Books
250 Sparks Avenue
Willowdale, Ontario
Canada M2H 2S4

Firefly Books (U.S.) Inc.
P.O. Box 1338
Ellicott Station
Buffalo, New York 14205

Printed and bound in Canada by:
D.W. Friesen & Sons
Altona, Manitoba

The Whales of Canada

By Erich Hoyt

Species Illustrations by Pieter A. Folkens

CAMDEN HOUSE

Contents

Whaling ship at Cape of Good Hope.

Introduction

The wind is up. Blowing in cold from the open North Pacific, it fills the sails that make our old wooden ketch creak and moan as it forges ahead. The blow curls the ocean as it breaks against the bow, even hurls the odd wave on deck — a fresh slap in the face, the better to stay alert, watching, waiting.

"Whales!" our guide yells. Three mottled grey bodies part the sea and erupt with shooting geysers — tall, straight spires that puncture the wind and float high above the waves.

"Whales!"

The cry is immediate and, at the same time, ancient — advertising, as forever, life at its grandest. For centuries, this cry signalled not life but oncoming death: With terrible certainty, an exploding harpoon would dispatch the animal, turning this marvel of life into a fast-bloating factory of meat and oil.

Our ideas about whales are changing. More and more people today consider whales friendly, intelligent and well worth keeping around. Scientists regard them as social mammals that took to the sea and adapted splendidly to oceanic life. Modern "whalers" hunt them not with harpoons but with cameras and a great deal of curiosity.

Sailing somewhere off British Columbia, we could be almost anywhere off Canada. These are grey whales, but they could be blues, belugas, humpbacks or killers. Since the close of commercial whaling in Canadian waters in the early 1970s, whales seem to be staging a modest recovery along this coastline, one of the world's longest, though perhaps we are just going out more often to look for them.

All of Canada's provinces and territories, except for landlocked Saskatchewan and Alberta, have cetaceans — the name scientists use for the whales, dolphins and porpoises. At least 20 species live along the shores and in the rivers of Canada, and perhaps another dozen species periodically visit Canada's three oceans. Cetaceans tend not to respect national boundaries.

Many cetaceans — particularly the toothed whales (odontocetes), which also include dolphins and porpoises — range widely in search of fish and squid. Most baleen whales (mysticetes) — the filter feeders that trap and strain small fish, krill and other marine invertebrates from the water with their baleen plates — undertake long annual migrations from warm temperate and tropical mating and calving waters to the cold temperate and polar feeding areas and back. Yet Canada is one of the few countries that provide a permanent home for certain species and, in some cases, much of the world population of a species:

• Thousands of belugas, or white whales, swim in and out of the northern rivers of Manitoba, Ontario, Quebec, the Northwest Territories and the Yukon, living in Canadian waters year-round.

• Bowhead whales spend their lives along the Arctic ice, following its retreat in the spring and dodging its advance in the fall, some remaining entirely within Canadian waters.

• Most of the world's narwhals, those long-tusked unicorns of the sea, reside in the deep waters of the eastern Canadian Arctic.

• Many North Atlantic fin and blue whales summer in the St. Lawrence River and the Gulf of St. Lawrence, while apparently wintering in the ice-free waters of the continental shelf off Nova Scotia.

• The resident killer whales of northern Vancouver Island — the densest concentration of killer whales anywhere in the world — probably spend all of the year in B.C. waters.

• Harbour porpoises in the northwest Atlantic and the northeast Pacific appear to have a limited inshore/offshore range, often entirely within Canadian waters. They are found throughout the northern hemisphere, but these puffing pigs, as Maritimers call them, have their world stronghold in the lower Bay of Fundy and the inshore waters of southwestern New Brunswick.

Cetaceans played an important role in Canada's early history and development. Long before Europeans arrived in the New World, Northwest Coast natives were featuring cetaceans in their art and legends. The Nootka Indians, among others, caught and ate them. The Inuit depended on harpooning marine mammals for survival. A beluga, narwhal or bowhead whale was a prize worth many seals.

In the 16th century, the first European explorers to Canada, told to scout for possible whaling and sealing grounds, quickly found them. Over the next two-plus centuries, whalers worked their way through the various large whales, exploiting each species in turn — roughly in order of size and accessibility — until it was gone or nearly gone. Commercial extinction is the point at which there are too few whales in a given area

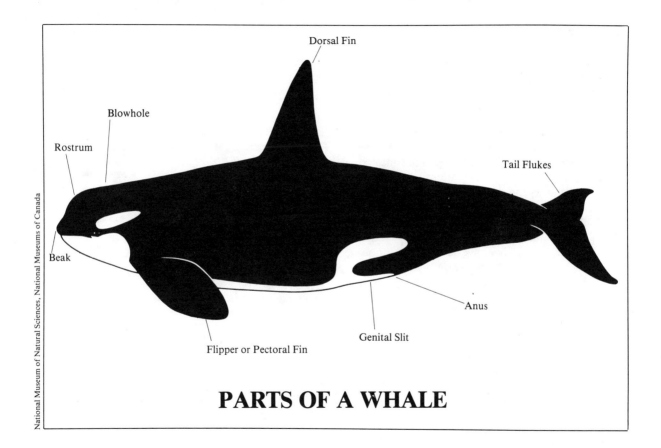

Dorsal Fin

Blowhole

Rostrum

Tail Flukes

Beak

Anus

Genital Slit

Flipper or Pectoral Fin

PARTS OF A WHALE

to bother pursuing them anymore. A few whales, of course, escaped the purge, but no one knows whether there are enough of some species to survive and re-populate.

By the late 1940s, Canada and other major whaling countries began sending biologists along on whaling expeditions. They examined whale carcasses on blood-slippery decks and at stinking whaling stations on-shore. They tried to learn as much as they could before the animal was rendered into oil. The data collected by these biologists helped conservationists to formu-late whaling quotas and eventually to convince some countries — such as Canada and the United States — to stop killing whales.

Since 1972, Canadian biologists have pioneered in the study of cetaceans. They have developed new non-lethal research methods to conserve the remaining whales. In the early 1970s, marine mammalogist Michael A. Bigg of the Department of Fisheries and Oceans in Nanaimo, British Columbia, photographed the nicks and other marks on the dorsal fins of killer whales to allow individual identification, and West Coast Whale Research Foundation zoologist James D. Darling photographed the uniquely scarred and pigmented backs of grey whales. Later, with several colleagues, Darling turned his camera on the tails of the humpbacks.

Identification studies enable scientists to determine population size and dynamics, migratory patterns and other movements plus reliable reproductive data, longevity, age at maturity, and birth and death rates.

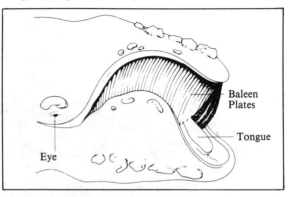

Baleen plates, which have the appearance of vertical venetian blinds, hang down from both sides of the roof of the whale's mouth. Each plate is fringed with bristles that act as a sieve to trap the small creatures on which the whale feeds.

University of British Columbia marine zoologist John K.B. Ford's discovery of dialects in killer whale pods was a first, since true local dialects are known only in humans and in a few other animals. Under-standing killer whale dialects allows Ford to analyze relationships among the pods and to monitor their movements using sound alone.

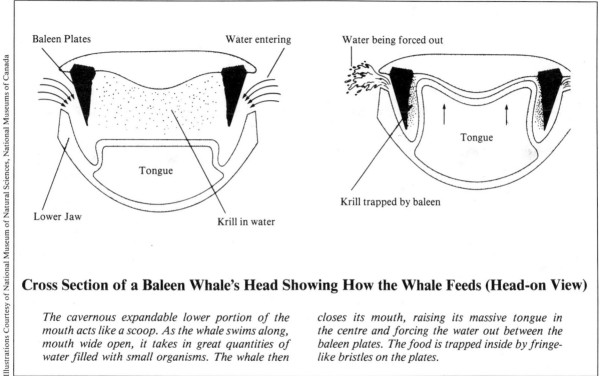

Illustrations Courtesy of National Museum of Natural Sciences, National Museums of Canada

Baleen Plates

Water entering

Water being forced out

Tongue

Krill in water

Lower Jaw

Krill trapped by baleen

Tongue

Cross Section of a Baleen Whale's Head Showing How the Whale Feeds (Head-on View)

The cavernous expandable lower portion of the mouth acts like a scoop. As the whale swims along, mouth wide open, it takes in great quantities of water filled with small organisms. The whale then closes its mouth, raising its massive tongue in the centre and forcing the water out between the baleen plates. The food is trapped inside by fringe-like bristles on the plates.

SHAPES AND SIZES

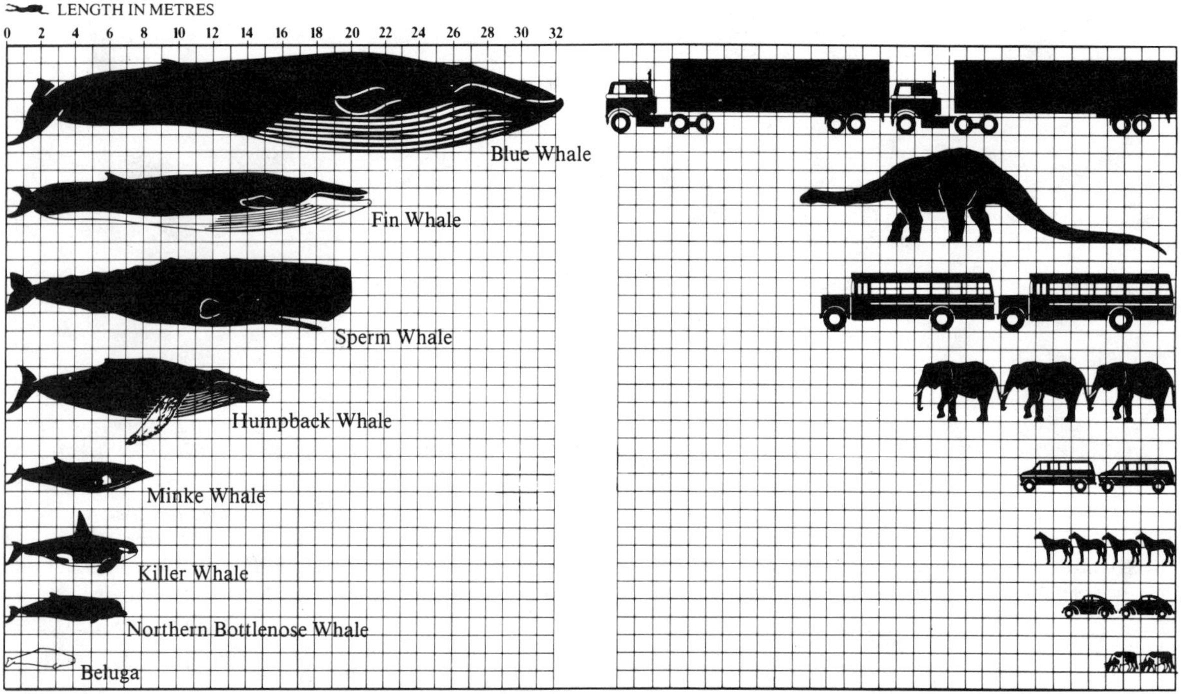

LENGTH IN METRES

0　2　4　6　8　10　12　14　16　18　20　22　24　26　28　30　32

Blue Whale

Fin Whale

Sperm Whale

Humpback Whale

Minke Whale

Killer Whale

Northern Bottlenose Whale

Beluga

National Museum of Natural Sciences, National Museums of Canada

Canadians have also led the way toward the conservation of the world's whales. The Greenpeace Foundation was born in Vancouver in 1970 with a mission to save the whales. Using the media to spread the message around the world, Greenpeace has become an international group with more than 500,000 members and offices in many countries. Other groups, such as the West Coast Whale Research Foundation, have made important, if less flamboyant, contributions, sometimes combining science with conservation. And a whole new industry has grown out of the research and conservation efforts: whale watching.

In 1971, Canada's first whale-watching cruise, conducted by the Montreal Zoological Society, went down the St. Lawrence in search of belugas and blue and fin whales. By the late 1970s, regular whale-watching tours were leaving from New Brunswick, Newfoundland, Nova Scotia, British Columbia, Quebec, Manitoba and the Northwest Territories. As of 1984, about 50 tour operators conduct regular whale-watching tours in Canada, with gross receipts exceeding $1 million.

How do whales react to so many voyeurs? There is little doubt that they are sometimes harassed by eager whale lovers — "hugged to death, almost," as one biologist put it. In 1983, the federal Department of Fisheries and Oceans tried to formulate preliminary guidelines for whale watching, though most whale-watching skippers are already extremely careful. As a result of whale watching, many more people care about cetaceans, and a little too much "hugging" is surely more welcome than a harpoon.

What is the future for cetaceans in Canada? Recent population studies of bowheads and narwhals in the Arctic reveal that current numbers are a little higher than previously estimated. But humpbacks, originally found in every strait and bay and along every stretch of North Pacific and North Atlantic shoreline, have failed to return in great number to B.C. waters. They are only beginning a slow comeback in the Maritimes. The northern right whale, once numerous, is even rarer today than the humpback. The chance of seeing a right whale off British Columbia is probably less than the chance of winning Lotto 6/49. Only 200 rights are believed to remain in the North Atlantic, many of these summering in the Bay of Fundy. No one knows whether there are enough right whales left to stage a real return. For these and other whales, dolphins and porpoises, scientists wonder what, if anything, can be done to help.

Perhaps the best thing we could do would be to stay out of their way — with our oil tankers, effluent outpourings, radioactive spills and nuclear tests.

As one scientist put it: "If we can't keep the whales alive and healthy, if we can't save the whales, how can we hope to save ourselves?"

GREY WHALE

Eschrichtius robustus

Grey Whale

Surfing With Devilfish

James D. Darling first noticed them during those endless summers in the early 1970s. His passion at the time was for riding a surfboard off Long Beach, on the west coast of Vancouver Island.

"The greys would come in to feed in the shallows," says Darling, "right behind the surf break, ploughing through the sand. You could see their sandy trails in the water. No one paid that much attention to them — except to make sure they weren't killer whales. We just kept on surfing, and they just kept on eating."

To support his surfing and his classes at the University of Victoria, Darling worked in the summer for Parks Canada at Pacific Rim National Park, then newly opened at Long Beach. Another summer, he drove a sea lion tour boat, "and we kept running into greys. But my first real work with them came in late 1972, when Parks Canada asked me to prepare a literature review of the species." Darling learned that grey whales weren't even supposed to be living off Vancouver Island in the summer but should have been thousands of miles north, feeding in the Bering Sea.

Then one night, Darling had dinner with David Hatler, a biologist conducting mammal surveys for Pacific Rim National Park and a sometime photographer of grey whales. As they talked of the greys they had seen, Darling mentioned one with an orange scar on the lower left side of its back. Hatler jumped up from the table and started rummaging through his

15

slides. He had photographed the same whale several years earlier. "I resolved right then to get a photograph of this orange-scarred whale," says Darling, "though of course I had no idea whether he'd return again."

Darling bought a 200mm telephoto lens for his camera and a 10-foot Zodiac inflatable. Whenever he was free of his park naturalist duties during the summer of 1973, he was whale-watching from the Zodiac. Eventually, he spotted the orange-scarred whale and got his shot. He took other photographs as well, including one of skin pigmentation patterns on a whale's back.

With their photographic proof in hand, Darling and Hatler coauthored a paper (published in 1974) reporting the presence of grey whales — some photographically identifiable — that return to Vancouver Island summer after summer.

"Using a camera to identify whales was a major revelation to me," recalls Darling. "At that time, I didn't know about Roger Payne's beginning efforts to identify southern right whales off Argentina."

Darling's work turned into a several-year study and a master's thesis at the University of Victoria. It was funded by the Vancouver Aquarium and Parks Canada plus Darling's unemployment insurance cheques and a university credit card for boat gas. In the winter of 1976-77, Darling interrupted his grey whale work to begin recording humpback songs off Maui, in the

Hawaiian Islands, but he returned to British Columbia in the spring. His thesis, "The Behaviour and Ecology of the Vancouver Island Grey Whales," was completed later that year.

With extensive photographic documentation, Darling estimated the summer resident population of grey whales at 26 in 1975 and 34 in 1976. Some individuals — like the orange-scarred grey — were seen in five successive summers. Darling's grey whales were clearly special. Each spring, most of the greys in the eastern North Pacific migrate along the coast from Mexico all the way to Alaska, but for eight months of the year, Darling's whales conveniently centred their activities near Pacific Rim National Park. Many of the Vancouver Island greys rejoined the migrators when they returned south in the fall and winter months, passing Vancouver Island en route to the mating and calving lagoons of Mexico.

In late summer 1982, a grey whale off Tofino (on the western shore of Vancouver Island) approached Darling's boat, rubbed along the side, then seemed to offer up its barnacle-encrusted head for scratching. When Darling and fellow researcher Beth Mathews patted it, the grey returned for more — every day for weeks. It began greeting other boats in the same way, and its behaviour caused a minor tourist boom in Tofino: It was a *friendly* grey whale.

In 1983, the Tofino friendly was nowhere to be found, but another friendly grey appeared, this time in Boundary Bay, south of Vancouver.

As grey whales come to live closer to humans, new problems arise. In spring 1984, nine grey whales in Puget Sound and in the Strait of Georgia washed up on the beaches — dead. An autopsy on one grey showed measurable contaminants in tissue samples. However, test results were not conclusive, mainly because no one knows what represents a dangerous contaminant level for whales.

The grey whale is one of the few success stories of whale conservation. There were perhaps as few as several hundred greys in the early 20th century, and now there are about 16,500 in the eastern North Pacific — believed to be close to original numbers.

With an expanding population acknowledged to be at or near the carrying capacity of its environment, it is inevitable that a few will arrive on the beaches. Yet some of the places where they are washing up — populated, polluted areas — are suspect.

More autopsies are needed, and there must be related water-quality studies before conclusions can be drawn. Doing these studies now might help to establish the contamination "danger levels" for grey whales. Too, grey whale difficulties may indicate much larger problems in the environment.

BIOLOGICAL PROFILE

The **GREY WHALE**, *Eschrichtius robustus*, is a baleen whale, Mysticeti, and is the only living member of the family of grey whales called Eschrichtiidae.

Size

Male grey whales average 40 to 50 feet long, though the females, slightly larger, sometimes reach 46 feet and weigh about 35 tons. Newborn calves measure 12 to 15 feet and are 1 to 1½ tons.

Features

Bulky and oddly tubular, grey whales taper at both ends and have a bowed, elongated head (V-shaped when viewed from above), 2 to 5 deep ventral grooves

Whaling boat overturned. Lithograph, 1858.

along the throat, small flippers with pointed tips and wide flukes separated by a median notch. They have no dorsal fin, just a low hump with ridges, or bumps — sometimes called knuckles — along the top of the tail stock. Colouring: mottled grey, with barnacles and white, yellow or orange patches, the result of concentrations of whale lice (cyamid crustaceans); calves are dark, with wrinkled skin and no barnacles. Adults may appear white or blue from the surface. The grey whale's blow is low (less than 12 feet) and puffy. Greys have 130 to 180 yellowish baleen plates (up to 10 inches long) on each side of the roof of the mouth, although those on the right-hand side are usually shorter due to the wearing action of predominantly right-side feeding. This right-mouthed feeding also produces more scars on the right side of the head. Many hollows, or pits, are located on top of the upper jaw, and most contain small, perhaps sensory, hairs.

Diet

Greys eat a wide variety of invertebrates, especially amphipods (tiny shrimplike crustaceans), bottom-dwelling isopods (free-swimming crustaceans), polychaetes (tube worms) and mysids (opossum shrimp). They feed in shallow water by grubbing along or near the bottom, sucking up food and expelling muddy trails that are often visible from the surface. They frequently swallow sand and rocks.

Natural History

Grey whales reach sexual maturity at about 36½ feet for males and 38 feet for females, when they are between 5 and 11 years of age. Between January and March, females give birth to a single calf in shallow southern lagoons after an 11-to-12-month gestation. Nursing lasts 6 to 9 months. There is a strong cow-calf bond, and mothers defend their calves aggressively, earning greys the name devilfish from whalers. In the lagoons, cows and calves segregate themselves from the males. Grey whales migrate close to shore and are seen alone or in groups of up to 16. Northern migration occurs in two distinct phases. The second group, which follows approximately 8 weeks after the first, is made up of cows and their calves. Natural enemies include killer whales, which feed on the tongues of greys, and large sharks, which may attack calves in addition to scavenging carcasses.

Range

Greys have one of the longest known annual migrations of any mammal. They winter in the lagoons of Baja California and Mexico and migrate to the Bering, Chukchi and western Beaufort Seas every summer. A few stop to feed along the coast of British Columbia and have been observed for much of the year off Vancouver Island.

Status

Grey whales have been protected by international agreement since 1946. Eastern North Pacific greys are believed at or near the carrying capacity of the environment — about 16,500 animals. The western North Pacific ("Korean") grey whale stock is very low, but exact numbers are unknown.

Minke Whale

The Camera-Shy Little Rorqual

Since 1980, zoologist Eleanor Dorsey has studied the little minke (pronounced "minky") whale in Canadian and U.S. waters. Assisted by A. Rus Hoelzel and S. Jonathan Stern, Dorsey has been sponsored by the World Wildlife Fund and the New York Zoological Society, for which she is a research fellow. Dorsey's winters are spent analyzing data at the Center for Long Term Research in Massachusetts, better known as The Payne Lab. Roger Payne's pioneering research with humpback and southern right whales has kept the place busy since the early 1970s. Every summer, Dorsey and her team head for the San Juan Islands off southern Vancouver Island.

She finds that minke whales can be individually identified by subtle natural marks and scars on their dorsal fins and by even more subtle pigmentation patterns on their flanks. Identifying individual animals is the key to learning more about any species. Dorsey has undertaken the task of photographing the minkes around southern Vancouver Island — 26 different minkes so far, and still counting.

Dorsey is calmly enthusiastic when she talks about her work, but when she goes into the field, she is fairly driven. Fellow Vancouver Island whale researcher Graeme Ellis, whose whale work has centred on the flamboyant humpback and killer whales, admires Dorsey: "You've got to be extremely determined to study minkes."

MINKE WHALE

Balaenoptera acutorostrata

Ellis once accompanied Dorsey in a 15-foot outboard motorboat off San Juan Island. Ellis's technique for getting identification shots has always been a blend of patience and persistence and a steady, unobtrusive way of approaching the animals — all finesse. But finesse doesn't work with minke whales.

For one thing, it is difficult to spot them. Minkes spend less time at the surface than humpbacks and killers. They surface to breathe from two to seven times in a row, but their spouts are almost invisible in the warm summer air of the San Juans. Then they disappear for 8 to 17 minutes. Also, minkes usually travel alone, so there is only one tiny black fin to look for in an expanse of ocean horizon. Finally, minkes are all business, lunge-feeding on small fish and krill throughout the summer. According to the anecdotal literature, the minke will sometimes swim alongside a ship, but in the waters around southern Vancouver Island, minkes seem to have little curiosity — and no interest in posing for pictures.

Dorsey describes her technique for photographing minkes: "You stand in the boat combing the sea for the first sign of a black fin. After a few hours or days [she has gone up to a month without sighting whales], a whale finally appears, and you race to the spot, camera ready. If you're *fast*, you'll reach the minke on the third or fourth blow and maybe get a good profile shot before it dives deep again. If you're *very fast*, you'll get there on the second blow and grab two or three profile shots."

After spending a white-knuckle start-and-stop afternoon with Dorsey chasing her minke whales, Ellis concluded: "Dorsey is *very fast*."

Summarizing four years of identification studies, Dorsey and her colleagues find that minkes, for the most part, like to stick to their own ranges — at least during the San Juan Islands' summer. Nine of the positively identified minkes are resident; they return every year. Another nine, seen only in one season, appear to be transients.

But Captain Hook, so named for a hooklike dorsal fin, doesn't fit the pattern of exclusive ranges within the San Juan Islands. Captain Hook regularly visits each of the three separate ranges.

Dorsey wonders what is different about Captain Hook. Could he be an amorous male visiting three different groups of females in far-flung ports? Mating probably occurs in winter, however, outside of Dorsey's study season. To find out whether sex has anything to do with the pattern of spatial use, she has been trying to sex minkes using skin samples. So far, the technique hasn't worked. Other whales are sexed from photographs of their bellies, but minkes rarely turn over at the surface, and photographing them in the murky underwater soup off the San Juans is nearly impossible.

One thing Dorsey has learned is that Captain Hook is a smart whale. Some minkes in Dorsey's study region feed by lunging or breaching through a school of fish, but Captain Hook comes up underneath flocks of birds, taking advantage of bait that is already concentrated. The birds are herring gulls, glaucous-winged gulls, common murres and rhinoceros auklets, and they usually hover over bunched-up schools of herring-sized fish — at least until Captain Hook arrives. Dorsey suspects that Captain Hook learned his eating habits from the bird-wise minkes in the southern part of her study area. The whales in the northern area are strictly lungers and breach-feeders, even when birds are advertising an easy feed. Despite Captain Hook's example, none of the northern minkes have copied his feeding behaviour.

In the summer of 1983, Dorsey visited Johnstone Strait off northern Vancouver Island and photographed the minkes that are sometimes seen feeding beside killer whales. Not one of them was a minke whale she knew from southern Vancouver Island, about 200 miles away, but she wonders if there is any exchange between the various ranges. The other big question is: Where do minkes go in winter? No one has yet discovered a winter mating and calving ground for minke whales in the North Pacific.

Minke whale research, a brand-new field, has important international implications. Minkes are not endangered in the world ocean, yet in the early 1980s — with blue, fin and sei whale stocks depleted — minkes became the most hunted baleen whale in the world. The majority of the whaling has occurred

around the Antarctic, where research is difficult and expensive. Eventually, Dorsey and her team want to study the Antarctic minkes. For now, however, the calm waters around southern Vancouver Island are ideal for learning the basics of minke biology and behaviour.

BIOLOGICAL PROFILE

The **MINKE WHALE**, *Balaenoptera acutorostrata*, is a baleen whale, Mysticeti, belonging to the family of rorqual whales called Balaenopteridae. The minke is also called pike whale, little piked whale, sharp-headed finner and, in Quebec, *petit rorqual*, *gibard* or *rorqual nain*.

Size

Minke whales measure 20 to 30 feet long, sometimes up to 35 feet, and weigh up to 10 tons. Calves are 8 to 9 feet at birth. Minkes are the smallest baleen whales in North American waters.

Features

Minke whales are streamlined, with an extremely narrow V-shaped head, a single head ridge, a tall curved dorsal fin, slim pointed flippers, broad flukes and 50 to 70 ventral grooves ending just behind the flippers. Sometimes a light chevron is visible behind the head. Colouring: grey to black back; lighter on flanks; white on belly and on underside of flippers and flukes; white band on top side of flippers is unique to minkes. The minke whale's blow is low and indistinct. Minkes have 230 to 360 yellowish baleen plates, each about 8 inches long. Some plates at the front of the mouth may have black streaks, while the posterior plates may be all dark.

Diet

Minkes feed on euphausiids (krill) and small shoal-ing fish, such as capelin, cod and herring. They sometimes breach or lunge-feed through schools of fish.

Natural History

Minke whales become sexually mature at 22 to 23 feet for males and 24 to 26 feet for females — at about 7 to 8 years of age. Females give birth every 1 to 2 years after a 10-to-11-month gestation. Calves nurse for 6 months or less. Although minkes are solitary animals, they sometimes appear in large groups — up to several hundred — on seasonal feeding grounds. Such groups may be segregated according to age and sex. Minke migration patterns are difficult to determine since they are widely distributed in all areas. Some minkes are known to stay in one area year-round. Minkes approach close to shore and enter bays, inlets and estuaries. They are occasionally preyed upon by killer whales.

Range

Minke whales range throughout the world ocean to the edge of the polar ice. In the summer, they are common off British Columbia and the Maritimes, including the Bay of Fundy, the St. Lawrence River and the Gulf of St. Lawrence.

Status

Because of their small size, minke whales were generally ignored by whalers — until recently. With many of the large whales endangered, the minke has become the most heavily harvested baleen whale in the world. They are still numerous in every ocean. The current estimated population in the North Atlantic is 130,000.

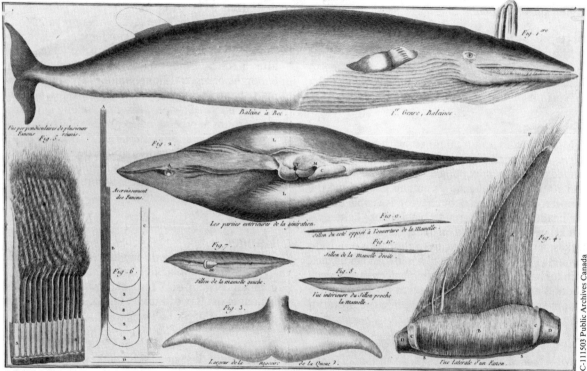

Minke whale. Line engraving by Benard.

Sei Whale

The Sprinter

The sei (pronounced "say") whale is something of an odd duck. If a biologist observed one off the North American continent, he would consider it an event, though the animals are not rare. The western North Atlantic population is estimated at 2,000, split chiefly between offshore Nova Scotia and Newfoundland/Labrador. But they reside *far* offshore, and they are elusive. At least, biologists have yet to isolate factors that may influence sei whale movements.

In the 19th century, Norwegian whalers and fishermen thought they had a clue. They named these whales *seje*, after the fish we call pollack, because sei whales would appear when fishermen made the first pollack catch of the season. Yet the whales weren't feeding on the pollack, and no one knew why they came in then. And even off Norway, the number of whales that appeared varied wildly.

The sei's reputation for elusiveness may stem from an identification problem. It looks like a small fin whale and is often identified as such — unless one confirms close up that the whale's lower lip and mouth cavity are not fin-whale white but sei-whale grey. Confusing the matter further are the sei's half-white baleen plates, occasionally visible near the front of its mouth. An experienced whaler recognized the sei immediately from its impressive sprinting speed and its erratic swimming pattern. The whale would zigzag to get away but, with all the endurance of a sprinter, would

SEI WHALE

Balaenoptera borealis

inevitably lose to the whaler. It is not known whether a sei would zigzag in response to the careful approach of a scientist or a whale watcher. Biologists William A. Watkins and William E. Schevill once identified a sei from the air, then watched it feed, abruptly changing directions as it swam near the surface.

Scientific knowledge about the sei whale is of fairly recent vintage. Whalers considered the sei — with its comparatively thin blubber and small size — a poor catch, until they ran out of blue and fin whales in the early 1960s. By the 1965-66 season, seis accounted for 72 percent of the total catch around the Antarctic, home of most of the world's whales. Between 1959 and 1971, an estimated 106,886 seis were killed — reducing them to about one-third of their original numbers. By 1974, the now-threatened sei whale stocks were finally studied; some of the basic population biology was determined from data that had been collected on all the carcasses. While sei whales are making a strong comeback in the Antarctic, very little is known about their natural history and their habits in the wild.

Peggy L. Edds of the University of Maryland is one of the few North American biologists to photograph living sei whales. She observed them while photographing fin whale scars and pigment patterns from a ship 60 miles west of Ocean City, Maryland, above the Baltimore Canyon, which is more than 100 fathoms deep. She is anxious to expand her fin whale identification study to include seis, but the erratic seis just haven't cooperated. One photography session won't make a study.

Of all the large whales, the sei may be the last to be researched by whale-watching scientists, the last to fall prey to the naturalist's eye.

BIOLOGICAL PROFILE

The **SEI WHALE**, *Balaenoptera borealis*, is a baleen whale, Mysticeti, belonging to the family of rorqual whales called Balaenopteridae. Quebeckers call it *rorqual boréal*.

Pursuit of a bowhead whale off Greenland. Woodcut, 1850.

Size

Male seis are 45 to 60 feet long, while the largest females range up to 69 feet; adults weigh up to 30 tons. Newborn calves are about 15 feet.

Features

Sei whales, sleek and streamlined, have a prominent curved dorsal fin — up to 2 feet high — relatively short pointed flippers, a single ridge along the top of the head and 32 to 60 well-defined ventral grooves. In profile, the head arches slightly downward toward the tip of the rostrum. Colouring: dark grey to black back, with wide variation; lighter belly, sometimes with pinkish tinge; right lower lip and mouth cavity are grey; white patches all over body are parasitic scars from lampreys and copepods. The blow of a sei whale is an inverted cone. Sei whales have 219 to 402 greyish black baleen plates on each side, the longest up to 2½ feet. The plates have fine, silky white fringes.

Diet

Sei whales eat euphausiids (krill), copepods (tiny planktonic crustaceans), squid and sometimes small fish. They are mainly skim-feeders, taking their prey near the surface and sometimes changing directions in successive feeding manoeuvres. They frequently leave a long pattern of swirls, or ripples, in the water during shallow feeding dives.

Natural History

Seis become sexually mature at 6 to 12 years of age. Every 2 to 3 years, after an 11-to-12-month gestation, cows give birth to a single calf. Calves usually nurse for 6 to 7 months. Sei whales generally travel in groups of 2 to 5. Larger concentrations are found on their feeding grounds. They undertake annual migrations, but their migratory movements are somewhat unpredictable. Capable of speed bursts of up to 30 miles per hour, seis were regarded by early whalers as the fastest-swimming rorqual.

Range

Sei whales range throughout the world ocean, especially in temperate seas. In the eastern North Pacific, they summer far off the B.C. coast; in the western North Atlantic, on the continental shelf off Nova Scotia and in the Labrador Sea. They stay well offshore in the northern hemisphere.

Status

Although not endangered, the North Pacific population — estimated at more than 10,000 — is considered depleted and is protected by the International Whaling Commission.

FIN WHALE

Balaenoptera physalus

Fin Whale

Asymmetry in the Whale World

Just as the symmetries of nature impress us with their grand and flawless designs, the asymmetries make us scratch our heads. Mathematicians shrug, muttering epithets about an imperfect world. Naturalists start theorizing and have a field day arguing with each other about how and why "it" got that way.

One of the most striking examples of asymmetry in the whale world is the fin whale. Even amateur whale watchers can identify a fin whale at sea — if they get a glimpse of the lower right side of the head. It is white — sometimes extending up as far as the right upper lip — while the entire left side is dark grey. Occasionally, there is a brush of greyish white sweeping up onto the back of the neck and the baleen plates on the front right side are white. The remaining 70 to 80 percent of the baleen plates on the right side — and all on the left — are striped with alternate bands of yellowish white and bluish grey. Inside the mouth and on the tongue, the grey/white arrangement is reversed, in a kind of "symmetry of asymmetry": the right side is pigmented or dark grey, while the left side is white. The rest of the fin whale's colour pattern is typical of many cetaceans: dark grey on the back and sides and white below, including the underside of both flippers and flukes.

Whale biologist Edward Mitchell of the Department of Fisheries and Oceans calls the fin whale's lopsided colour pattern "countershading," with the colours on the head having been rotated 90 degrees from the usual cetacean colour pattern. This might be useful in feeding strategies. The fin whale sometimes circles a school of fish, turning on its side as it opens its mouth. Naturalists who have seen fin whales moving in a counterclockwise motion say that the dark area facing the fish functions as camouflage. Those who have seen the clockwise move suggest that the whales are startling — perhaps herding — the fish by flashing the white area. Fin whales may use both of these moves — depending on circumstances — or neither. This will only be determined when some patient whale watcher methodically tests the various theories.

Beginning in the late 1960s, Mitchell went to sea, counting live fin whales and sampling fresh carcasses provided by whalers. He estimates that there are about 7,200 fin whales around Newfoundland and Nova Scotia. He found that the main summer feeding area lies between the shore and the 1,000-fathom curve running from Massachusetts to Labrador.

In the 1970s, U.S. biologists William E. Schevill and William A. Watkins recorded fin whales that were feeding. They were making low-pitched pulsed sounds, at 20 Hz, below the level of human hearing. Another fin whale can hear the sounds up to 15 miles away. While Schevill and Watkins watched and listened, more fin whales swam in and joined the feeders. Accidentally or intentionally, they had been "called" to the feeding site.

Since then — as part of intensive whale research programmes in Canada and the eastern United States — fin whales are being photographically identified by pigment and dorsal fin markings. Richard Sears

spends time with fin whales in the St. Lawrence River when he isn't busy with blues, though his associate Mary Pratt is currently planning a fin whale ID study. Hal Whitehead and other researchers off Newfoundland have concentrated on humpbacks but are beginning to look at fins. Charles "Stormy" Mayo, Steven Katona and other U.S. biologists who work with humpback whales from Cape Cod to Maine prefer humpback research but do photograph the fin whales that present themselves. Only U.S. biologist Peggy L.

Edds, working off Maryland, has focused on fin whales, though she is currently not doing any fieldwork.

Many whale watchers and even naturalists working the North Atlantic tend to yawn when fin whales are sighted. Herman Melville found fin whales more elusive than boring, but his comments in *Moby-Dick* help illuminate the historical lack of interest:

"Of a retiring nature, he eludes both hunters and philosophers. Though no coward, he has never yet shown any part of him but his back, which rises in a long, sharp ridge. Let him go. I know little more of him, nor does anybody else."

Eventually, speedy boats did catch up with the fin whale, yet today, we know little more of the animal's life than Melville did. But, thanks in part to its intriguing asymmetry, the fin whale is beginning to work on man's curiosity.

BIOLOGICAL PROFILE

The **FIN WHALE**, *Balaenoptera physalus*, is a baleen whale, Mysticeti, belonging to the family of rorqual whales called Balaenopteridae. The fin is also called finback, finner and, in Quebec, *rorqual commun*.

Size

Fin whales measure up to 88 feet for the largest females, but most males and females are 60 to 70 feet long and weigh up to 50 tons. Calves are 20 to 21 feet at birth and about 2 tons.

Features

Slender and elongated, fin whales have a tall curved dorsal fin, a narrow, flat V-shaped head and up to 100 slim ventral grooves extending to the navel. They also have a distinctly ridged back from dorsal fin to flukes, earning them the name razorback. Colouring: dark back, white underside except for head, which tends to be white on right side — especially lower part, but sometimes upper lip and baleen — and dark grey on left side; baleen is white in right front and, elsewhere, streaked with yellowish white and bluish grey; pale greyish white chevrons sometimes visible on back. A fin whale's blow is a tall inverted cone up to about 20 feet high. Fin whales have 260 to 480 baleen plates per side, each about 2 feet long and edged with grey bristles.

Diet

Fin whales eat euphausiids (krill), pelagic crustaceans and a wide variety of fish (sand lance, herring, capelin, cod and pollack).

The Era *preparing for spring whaling. Fullerton, N.W.T., May 1904.*

Natural History

Fin whales reach sexual maturity at about 58 feet (males) and 60 feet (females), when they are between 6 and 12 years of age. Every 2 or 3 years, cows give birth to a single calf after an 11-to-12-month gestation. Calves nurse for about 7 months. Most fins migrate northward in spring and toward the equator in fall, although some northern-hemisphere fins move inshore in winter. They travel in pods of 6 or 7 but are often seen singly or in pairs; several pods may concentrate in a small area. Fin whales are deep divers — sometimes reaching depths of at least 750 feet. They are also fast swimmers, capable of speed bursts of more than 20 miles per hour. Fin whales produce sporadic low-frequency sounds that can be heard up to 15 miles away and have been known to attract other fin whales to a specific feeding site. Fin whales are occasionally attacked by killer whales.

Range

Fin whales prefer the deep waters of the world ocean, but there are sizable inshore concentrations in eastern Canada, including the St. Lawrence River and the Gulf of St. Lawrence as well as the lower Bay of Fundy.

Status

As blue whale populations declined in the 1950s, whalers turned their attention to fins, and soon, fin whale numbers had dropped drastically. They are now protected to the extent that large-scale whaling of fins has stopped. The world population is estimated to be 200,000, mostly in the southern ocean.

BLUE WHALE

Balaenoptera musculus

Blue Whale

Old Sulphur-Bottom

At up to 100 feet long and an estimated 150 tons, the blue whale is the largest creature ever known to have lived on Earth.

Yet, says Richard Sears modestly, *"our* blues aren't that big." He and colleagues J. Michael Williamson and Frederick Wenzel have been studying blue whales in the St. Lawrence River and the Gulf of St. Lawrence since 1979. Sears estimates the size of the largest ones that have glided by his rubber inflatable at around "six boat lengths," or 80 to 85 feet and a mere 80 tons — equal in mass to 15 to 20 African elephants.

Sears, an American born in Paris, has learned to speak French like a Quebecker, which is handy when working out of a tiny village on the north shore of the Gulf of St. Lawrence. He has won research contracts from Hydro-Québec and Parks Canada and leads whale-watching tours for part of the year, working on a shoestring budget the rest of the time with the energetic support of a close-knit team.

Every year from August through October, Sears and his colleagues follow and photograph the whales, dolphins and porpoises of Quebec. When they spot a blue, they stay with it as long as they can. Since 1981, they have been using high-resolution photography to identify individual blues. Their technique is similar to that used by researcher Eleanor Dorsey on minke whales. Blue whales, like minkes, have unique pigmentation patterns on their sides and backs. Yet blues, much larger, are even more mottled, and that makes photo-identification generally easier, though the blues are scarcer and range over much wider areas.

Sears has photographed blue whales feeding on swarms of tiny shrimplike krill in an unusual sequence he calls "arc-and-roll feeding." Says Sears: "The blue comes lunging up from below and surfaces on its back. The tail is arched downward, and all you see is this gigantic ventral pouch all distended as it breaks the surface."

The pouch is filled with tons of water and food. As the whale begins to expel the water from its mouth, straining the food from it, "the blue rolls on its belly, spouts and inhales a deep breath." During several shallow dives, as the blue surfaces up to four times in three minutes, its mouth stays open, still expelling

water. By the final dive, the pouch is collapsed, and the whale swallows its catch.

The blue whale can hardly do anything without getting its name in the record books. Basic reproduction biology stretches the imagination. Newborn calves are 23 feet long and weigh 5,500 pounds. In a 24-hour period, they devour more than 50 gallons of milk, gaining about 200 pounds of weight daily, or 8 pounds an hour. When weaned, at 8 months, the calf is 50 feet long and about 50,000 pounds — larger than all but a few species of whales at maturity.

Sears and his team have identified some 60 individual blue whales but believe there may be as many as a hundred along the north shore of the Gulf of St. Lawrence. Some return in successive years — so far, up to three years in a row. Many range close to land, concentrating in several areas.

There are a mere 11,200 blue whales left in the world, and those off Quebec, accessible for study, may be crucial to the survival of the rest.

BIOLOGICAL PROFILE

The **BLUE WHALE**, *Balaenoptera musculus*, is a baleen whale, Mysticeti, belonging to the family of rorqual whales called Balaenopteridae. Blues are also called sulphur-bottoms and, in Quebec, *rorqual bleu* or *baleine bleue*.

Blue whale beached on Anticosti Island, Quebec.

Size

The largest recorded size for a blue whale (a female Antarctic blue) is about 100 feet long and more than 150 tons, but the average size is 70 to 85 feet and 90 to 125 tons. Newborn calves are about 23 feet long and 5,500 pounds. At 8 months, calves are 50 feet long and weigh 50,000 pounds — larger than most species of whales at maturity. The blue whale is probably the biggest animal ever to live on this planet, even surpassing the dinosaurs.

Features

Blues are long and streamlined, with a relatively small (1-foot-high) dorsal fin, long pointed flippers, broad straight-edged flukes and a wide flat head with one median ridge. Fifty-five to 68 ventral grooves extend to the navel. The blowholes are protected by large, fleshy "splash guards" that appear to contract and expand as the animal breathes. Colouring: mottled bluish grey; the yellowish hue on the belly of some animals is due to accumulations of diatoms (algae) in colder water — whalers used to call them sulphur-bottoms. A blue whale's slender, vertical blow can reach 30 feet. There are 270 to 395 short, stiff, black baleen plates, each up to 3 feet long, on both sides.

Natural History

Males become sexually mature at about 74 feet, females at 79 feet, or roughly 10 years of age. Cows give birth to a single calf once every 2 to 3 years. Gestation lasts approximately 12 months, and calves nurse for about 8 months. Blues are solitary animals but sometimes travel in pairs. They may be found in larger, though well-spaced, concentrations on rich feeding banks. In spite of their impressive size, blue whales are sometimes attacked and killed by killer whales.

Diet

The blue whale, a relatively shallow feeder, can devour 6 to 8 tons of euphausiids (krill) in one day.

Range

Blue whales range throughout the world ocean, mainly along continental shelves and ice fronts but also in shallow inshore regions and in the deep ocean. They can be reliably seen off the north shore of the Gulf of St. Lawrence from August to October.

Status

Blue whales are endangered. The world population is estimated at 11,200, a fraction of their original numbers. About 500 are believed to remain in the western North Atlantic and 1,700 in the North Pacific. Protected by the International Whaling Commission since 1966, they may be making a slow recovery in some areas.

Humpback Whale

Not-So-Gentle Giant

In an annual ritual practised by many Canadians, North American humpback whales summer in northern latitudes and winter in the south. East Coast humpbacks spend their winters in the Caribbean. West Coasters, like their Canadian human counterparts, travel to Mexico and Hawaii. How do researchers know this?

Humpbacks flip their tails in a kind of final salute before making a deep dive. Their tail flukes are wonderfully variegated in black-and-white patterns, ranging from nearly all white to all black. As with snowflakes and fingerprints, no two humpback tails are alike.

Since the mid-1970s, Canadian and U.S. researchers have photographed some 2,000 different tails in the North Atlantic and about 1,000 in the North Pacific. These photographs have provided proof of the humpback migration by showing the same individuals in both the summer and winter homes. In a few cases, the photographs revealed that a specific individual wintered off Hawaii one year and off Mexico the next. In addition, the long and complex song of the Mexican humpbacks is the same as that sung by Hawaiian humpbacks, leading researchers to an inescapable conclusion: the eastern and central North Pacific is occupied by a single population of humpback whales.

These and other findings about humpback whales have come from a recently completed five-year study

HUMPBACK WHALE

Megaptera novaeangliae

headed by Canadian zoologist James D. Darling, with U.S. zoologists Roger Payne and Peter Tyack. For several summers, Darling lived with grey whales off the west coast of Vancouver Island, where he first saw humpbacks. But whalers had wiped out all but a few relatively inaccessible humpbacks on the B.C. coast, and in order to really study them, Darling had to go to Hawaii. He could have gone to Alaska, of course, but his first humpback job — recording their songs — could only be done in the warm winter breeding areas of Mexico or Hawaii. North Pacific humpbacks rarely sing in the summer feeding areas off Alaska and British Columbia. Hawaii is the more popular wintering area because the water is warmer, calmer and clearer. It is one of the best places in the world to study humpbacks or any species of whale.

Besides recording the underwater songs in Hawaii, Darling began the photographic identification of humpback tails and made observations of their behaviour. In 1980, Darling helped assemble a team of Canadian and U.S. researchers to do a major two-year study and obtained substantial funding from the National Geographic Society, the Clifford E. Lee Foundation of Canada and the World Wildlife Fund of Canada and the United States. It was one of the biggest whale-behaviour studies ever conducted, and it not only increased our knowledge about humpbacks but also altered the way we look at all whales.

The big change can be traced to a sunny, calm day late in the winter of 1979. Cruising off Maui in their open motorboat, Darling and fellow researcher Gregory K. Silber were showing off Hawaii's "gentle giants" to a *Paris Match* reporter. The whales were swimming along peacefully, a cow and calf followed by what the researchers called an "escort" — an adult that often accompanied a cow and calf — and finally, trailing somewhat farther behind, two other adults. One of the pleasures on such an extremely calm day was a chance to view the whales underwater. As Darling eased the Boston Whaler close to the whales, Silber put on his face mask and leaned over the side, his face in the water. Seconds later, he jerked up his head, yelling: "One whale just hit the other!" Silber had seen the escort leave the cow and calf and rush back and hit one of the other adults.

Darling couldn't believe it.

He grabbed the face mask and watched as the escort appeared to block the other two adults to keep them from approaching the cow. The escort blew a stream of bubbles from its blowhole, forming a silvery wall that temporarily obscured the cow and the calf from view. Leaving the side of the cow and calf, the escort swam below one of the other adults, rolled on its side and lashed its tail at the whale, striking a glancing blow. Then, in the bubbling-water turbulence, the escort sidled back to the cow and calf. The tail —

45

often studded with hard, jagged barnacles — is a whale's most powerful weapon. Darling saw blood on the escort's tail and on the other adult's back — superficial wounds, but marks of a clear message sent. Darling, Silber and the reporter traded the face mask back and forth for several hours, fascinated. "Not exactly gentle giants!" recalls Darling. "We'd caught

these supposedly docile, peace-loving animals beating the tar out of each other."

A week later, on another flat, calm day, Darling and company saw more violence and blood. But this time, after hours of fighting, one of the trailing adults changed places with the escort. It was as if it had *won* the position of honour.

Darling and the others wanted to learn the signifi-

cance of the aggression. But that was to take most of two more field seasons. The escorts were thought to be females, aunties that helped with the child rearing. It was an understandable notion if one assumed that humpbacks were like bottlenose dolphins. But why would humpbacks fight for the honour of being an auntie? It didn't make sense. To explain it, Darling needed more data; he needed to know the identity, and particularly the sex, of all the animals involved.

Few researchers had even tried to sex humpback whales. One method was to see — or, better yet, to photograph — the genital slit and anus. The position varies slightly from male to female. Humpback whales' genitals are rarely exposed to view at the surface. Darling worked with diving photographer Flip Nicklin and fellow researchers to develop a technique. One by one, they sexed and identified many of the whales, including the elusive "singers" that sang alone at depths of 60 feet or more. Slowly, as they obtained a profile of some 81 whales, the real story emerged:

The escorts, the other adults and the singers are *all* males. At certain times, a given male will be a singer. But on another day, he may become one of the "other adults," and his goal was to become an escort, a dominant male. The singing may be a way to win a female without a fight. It is possible that the best singer earns some advantage when it comes to mating. And perhaps the singers unable to resolve matters in the recording studio are the ones that take to fighting over access to a female that is obviously, as Darling says, "in heat or about to come into heat."

Like many other scientists and whale lovers of the 1960s and early 1970s, Darling was attracted to these large-brained, almost mystical singers of the deep. Gradually, his hard research and careful observations began to strip away the mystery. With their infighting, apparent dominance hierarchies and mating strategies, humpbacks and other whales are turning out to be remarkably like land mammals. From creatures that once crawled upon the land, whales have made some incredible and intriguing oceanic adaptations. Being able to study whales comparatively — as social mammals — is providing a key to understanding their mystery.

BIOLOGICAL PROFILE

The **HUMPBACK WHALE**, *Megaptera novae-angliae*, is a baleen whale, Mysticeti, belonging to the family of rorqual whales called Balaenopteridae. In Quebec, the humpback is called *rorqual à bosse* or *baleine à bosse*.

Size
Humpbacks can measure up to 53 feet long but are usually only 38 to 43 feet. They may weigh 40 tons.

Calves are about 15 feet long and 1½ tons at birth.

Features
Humpbacks are robust, with a small dorsal hump and/or fin, long winglike flippers (up to 16 feet, almost one-third of body length), distinctive head knobs of varying sizes, a rounded protuberance near the tip of the lower jaw and 14 to 35 broad ventral grooves. They are frequently covered with whale lice (cyamid crustaceans) and barnacles. Colouring: black, with white patches on flippers and on underside of body, especially the flukes, which are variegated in black-and-white patterns. Because no two humpback tails look alike, they are used to identify individual animals. The humpback has a thick, bushy, balloon-shaped blow up to 10 feet high. Humpbacks have 300 to 400 black baleen plates, each about 2 to 2½ feet long, growing from each side of the roof of the mouth. Humpback baleen is edged with black or olive-black bristles.

Diet
Humpback whales feed on schooling fish (herring, sand lance, capelin, mackerel, codfish and salmon), euphausiids (krill) and crustaceans, often using "bubble nets," or "bubble clouds," to concentrate their prey and then charging through the column, mouths open wide.

Forty-ton humpback whale being towed up a ramp at Coal Harbour, British Columbia, 1948.

Natural History

Male humpbacks reach sexual maturity at 36 to 39 feet, females at 37 to 41 feet. Every 1 to 3 years or more, after an 11-to-12-month gestation, cows give birth to a single calf. Newborn calves have a wrinkly appearance. Nursing sometimes lasts for more than a year. In the winter breeding and calving grounds, a cow and her calf stay together, accompanied at times by an escort. Escorts are males apparently waiting for the females to come into oestrus. Escorts and other males jockey with each other for this position, and there are sometimes bloody skirmishes at the surface. Only male humpbacks "sing," and they sing alone, but singers may eventually fight and become escorts. The songs — several themes arranged in a long series of repeated phrases — are apparently specific to separate populations and may vary slightly from one year to the next. They are considered the longest and most complex songs in the animal kingdom. Humpbacks undertake extensive seasonal migrations and generally prefer shallow banks and shelf waters. Although they are often found alone or in small groups, aggregations of 200 or more have been observed on feeding grounds. Humpback whales are not usually fast swimmers, but they are active and acrobatic, often breaching or lying on their sides, smacking the surface with their tails (lobtailing) or flippers (flippering). They raise their flukes high into the air before making a long, deep dive. They are sometimes attacked by killer whales, though the incidence of bite marks on healthy humpbacks indicates that many attacks are not fatal. Death probably comes more often from entanglement in fishing nets, especially in inshore areas off eastern Canada.

Range

Humpbacks range throughout the world ocean, spending their winters breeding in subtropical nearshore waters and their summers feeding in cold temperate waters.

Status

Humpbacks are an endangered species. Because of their preference for near-shore areas, humpback numbers were severely depleted by shore-based whalers. Although they have been given worldwide protection since 1966, their recovery has been slow. Current world population is estimated at 8,000 to 10,000, of which roughly 3,000 reside in the western North Atlantic and 2,000 in the eastern North Pacific.

BOWHEAD WHALE

Balaena mysticetus

Bowhead Whale

Skirting the Arctic Ice

Every major whale species has a unique horror story about whaling, but the bowhead's nightmare rivals the worst. From the 17th to the early 20th century, the bowhead was the object of a hunt so far-ranging and thorough that not even near extinction would end the siege. Along with the closely related right whale, the bowhead (then known as the Arctic right whale) was considered the "right" one to kill. Both whales move slowly and are unaggressive; both are rich in oil and baleen and offer blubber so thick (up to 28 inches) that, unlike most other species, they float when killed.

For three centuries, the bowhead and the right were the equivalent of a petroleum and plastics industry. Their oil lit lamps in houses, factories and churches and along streets; it was turned into lubricant for machinery; it was used to manufacture soap, paint and rope. The bowhead's baleen was a special prize, even more valuable than the right's. Up to 14 feet in length, bowhead baleen is the longest of any whale's. Made of keratin, baleen is a strong yet light substance growing from the roof of the mouth in two rows of comb-like plates, which allow the bowhead to strain krill, planktonic crustaceans and other organisms from the water. Baleen was mainly used in the manufacture of corset and dress stays, umbrella ribs, fishing rods and buggy whips. A bowhead might contain a ton of baleen, which sold for $5 a pound in the late 19th century. Sometimes the profit from one bowhead could finance a year's whaling voyage. The invention of spring steel in 1906 sent the price of baleen crashing — from $5 to 50 cents a pound overnight. Bowhead whaling collapsed; unfortunately, the species had nearly collapsed by then too.

Bowheads spend their lives at the edge of the Arctic ice. They follow its retreat in the summer, penetrating the high latitudes to feed. They remain until the fall, when the newly forming ice drives them south, but they never leave the Arctic. They were once found throughout the northern circumpolar region, but now, most bowheads live in the Bering and Chukchi Seas off Alaska and in the Beaufort Sea, the so-called western Arctic of Canada. In Hudson Bay and Foxe Basin, fewer than a hundred are left. In Baffin Bay and Davis Strait, estimates range to several hundred. In the Greenland and Barents Seas, where European bowhead whaling began, they may be entirely gone.

For the last few summers, biologist Bernd Würsig of the Moss Landing Marine Laboratories in California has investigated bowhead behaviour in the Beaufort Sea. Watching from the air, from shore and from a variety of boats, Würsig and several colleagues learned that the whales alternated between periods of socializing and long bouts of intensive feeding. The Würsig group was the first to report a bowhead surfacing with mud in its mouth, an indication of bottom-feeding. They also saw bowheads skim-feeding at the surface, but most of the feeding, particularly in the 1981-82 field seasons, occurred in the water column.

The bowhead feeding strategy depended on the kind of prey and its behaviour. For example, bowheads sometimes feed cooperatively — probably to take efficient advantage of dense swarms of invertebrates.

Würsig and his colleagues saw up to 14 whales swimming at the surface, staggered behind and to the side of each other in U-shaped echelons. All moved in the same direction and at the same speed, their mouths wide open.

The most recent bowhead population counts are up, allowing for cautious optimism. According to a four-year average for 1978-82, there are from 2,500 to 3,800 bowheads in the western Arctic.

But intensive studies continue — in an effort to determine current and potential harassment to bowheads from tanker traffic, offshore oil rigs, pollution of every kind and native hunting. The latter continues on a limited basis today and, despite strict controls, may be jeopardizing a real comeback.

There is no question that Arctic development will increase. Natives, scientists and even representatives from government and from oil companies agree that we should include bowheads in the future of the Arctic. But no one really knows if that is a long-range possibility. Can we proceed slowly enough and in such a way that we are not burning our ecological bridges? Having barely survived the whaling era, the bowhead faces an uncertain future.

BIOLOGICAL PROFILE

The **BOWHEAD WHALE**, *Balaena mysticetus*, is a baleen whale, Mysticeti, belonging to the family of right whales called Balaenidae. Quebeckers call it *baleine boréale* or *baleine franche du Groenland*.

Size

Bowhead whales are usually about 57 feet long, but the largest measured female was 65 feet. They weigh up to 100 tons. Calves are 13 to 15 feet at birth.

Features

Bowheads are very stocky and have a huge, triangular head (one-third of the total body length) with a highly bowed lower jaw (from which they derive their name), a rounded back with no dorsal fin and broad spatulate flippers. An indentation, or dip, behind the blowholes is noticeable when they surface. Their skin is smooth with no barnacles, and they have no ventral grooves. Colouring: all black except for white chin patch with grey or black spots and sometimes a white belly patch; there is a greyish stripe around the tail stock. Because the blowholes are widely separated, the bowhead has a distinctly V-shaped blow. Bowheads have 230 to 360 long, narrow, dark grey baleen plates on each side. Each baleen plate has fine, black or grey bristles.

Diet

Bowheads eat euphausiids (krill), amphipods (tiny shrimplike crustaceans) and copepods (tiny planktonic crustaceans). Although they are mainly skim-feeders, they also take food in the water column and at or near the bottom in shallow regions, at which time their movements can be tracked from their muddy trails. Groups of up to 14 bowheads sometimes feed cooperatively. Staggered behind and to the side of each other in U-shaped echelons, they move in the same direction, at the same speed, with their mouths wide open.

Head of humpback whale. Snooks Arm, Notre Dame Bay, Newfoundland, 1910.

Natural History

Bowhead males reach sexual maturity at about 38 feet, females at 40 feet, or at approximately 4 years of age. Cows probably calve mostly between March and August after an estimated 13-month gestation. They give birth at intervals of 2 years or more. Calves nurse for about a year. Bowhead whales usually travel alone or in groups of no more than 6. Loose aggregations of 50 or more are sometimes observed on feeding grounds or when ice has forced them into a restricted area. Although bowheads are migratory, their movements are dictated by advancing and retreating ice. During migration, they tend to segregate themselves according to age and sex. Bowheads are relatively slow-moving and unaggressive and alternate between periods of socializing and long bouts of intensive feeding. They can remain submerged for more than 40 minutes but are probably not deep divers. Bowheads have been known to hang vertically in the water with only their heads visible and also to smack the surface with their tails (lobtailing) and flippers (flippering). Bowheads are preyed upon by killer whales.

They are also sometimes at the mercy of ice that forms or shifts quickly. If feeding areas become inaccessible, the whales may starve, or they may become trapped and suffocate.

Range

Bowhead whales range along pack ice of the Arctic. Most live in the Bering, Chukchi and Beaufort Seas, especially off Alaska. They are pushed south by advancing ice in winter and follow the retreating ice in summer.

Status

Bowhead whales were hunted to near extinction from the 17th to the early 20th century. They are still harvested by natives in a few coastal villages in northern Alaska, and there are plans to expand this fishery. There are an estimated 2,500 to 3,800 bowheads in the western Arctic. In Hudson Bay and Foxe Basin, fewer than a hundred remain; in Baffin Bay and Davis Strait, estimates range to several hundred.

NORTHERN RIGHT WHALE

Eubalaena glacialis

Northern Right Whale

Lonely Survivor

Extinction is a touchy subject when one is talking about the northern right whale — called "right" because it was the right, or preferred, one for a whaler to catch. Long gone is the world that once harboured tens of thousands of right whales in every ocean. The few hundred northern right whales alive today have never known a time when they weren't fighting for their biological lives. They are lonely survivors.

The right whale has been protected from whaling for nearly half a century. Yet according to the best estimates — roaring guesses, really — there are 220 in the vast North Pacific and 200 in the North Atlantic. Another 3,000 *southern* right whales inhabit the southern hemisphere, but they are geographically separate and, though they look the same, are considered a distinct species by many taxonomists.

Why are the rights not recolonizing old habitats, as the greys have done or as the humpbacks seem to be doing in some areas? Scientists are afraid that there may simply be too few left and that humans may have taken over prime right habitats. Under such circumstances, their low birth rate may preclude any significant population increase.

In the midst of such a bleak outlook, the recent discovery that a group of right whales regularly summers in the lower Bay of Fundy has been cause for celebration among whale watchers and scientists. On July 10, 1980, American biologists Randall R. Reeves,

Scott D. Kraus and Porter Turnbull were flying over Fundy conducting a cetacean inventory when they encountered their first right whales. In subsequent weeks, they saw many more — up to 19 in one four-hour period. By taking photographs of the unique whitish patches, called callosities, found on the head of every right whale, they could distinguish 26 different rights, including four cow/calf pairs. The right whales were present from July through October and could usually be found in the lower Fundy, along the 100-fathom line where they were feeding on tiny planktonic crustaceans called copepods.

In the summer of 1981, Reeves, Kraus and Turnbull continued their inventory, hoping that the rights would return to be counted. They spent as much time as possible on the water in their 30-foot motorboat and met 59 individual whales — some of them returnees — including seven cow/calf pairs. Initially, they were elated by the apparent productivity. However, they later learned that calves may remain with their mothers for more than a year; thus calf sightings from one year to the next are not always new ones.

The researchers also witnessed apparent sexual activity. Since right whales supposedly mate and conceive only in midwinter, they questioned what they were seeing. Some of the sexual activity involved pairs, but much of it was group sex: a tangled array of massive black bodies churning the water. This could be courtship behaviour, or it might be all in play. There is no hard evidence that mating leading to conception is occurring.

As the right whale story spread, other researchers were on the lookout for rights. In 1982, there were 69 individual right whales identified in the Bay of Fundy and another 45 on Browns Bank, south of Nova Scotia. No calves accompanied this latter group, perhaps because the area is out to sea and more vulnerable to shipping traffic.

After the 1982 season, Kraus and John H. Prescott of Boston's New England Aquarium assembled all of the right whale identification photographs taken by researchers working the coast from New Brunswick to Cape Cod. By comparing callosity patterns, Kraus and Prescott were able to show that right whales travel back and forth between these areas — not only from year to year but also within a season. Thus the right whales from Browns and Baccaro Banks off Nova Scotia, Georges Bank off Massachusetts, and the Gulf of Maine all belong to the Fundy stock.

How did the Bay of Fundy right whales escape the notice of biologists for so long? They didn't, entirely. As early as 1965, the captain and crew of the *Bluenose* ferry, which sails from Bar Harbor, Maine, to Yarmouth, Nova Scotia, spotted 15 rights. Scientists, however, took little notice — they doubted the *Bluenose* report. The first biologists to verify the presence of right whales and to recognize the significance of such sightings were David E. Gaskin and his associates at the University of Guelph. In the early 1970s, Gaskin and his team were studying harbour porpoises off southwestern New Brunswick when they encountered a few right whales. It took awhile for the import of this discovery to sink in: Fundy was probably the right whales' last stand, the summer home of much of the entire North Atlantic population.

But how had whalers missed the right whales in the Bay of Fundy? There are a few musty records of whaling voyages there, but Fundy seems to have been rarely visited in the heyday of whaling, probably because of terrible tides and unrelenting summer fogs. So the rights and other cetaceans have persisted there, a remnant population surviving only a few hundred miles from what was once the nerve centre of New England Yankee whaling.

Yet these chance-protected rights have not completely escaped the influence of man. In the growing traffic and intensive development of the Atlantic Seaboard, the right whale is being crowded out. Man's plans for Fundy include tidal-power projects, a nuclear power plant at Point Lepreau, New Brunswick, and an oil refinery and marine terminal at Eastport, Maine. Probably the biggest threat is the tanker traffic, with the risk of oil spills.

Without Fundy, the northern right whale, at least in the North Atlantic, might well be extinct. Fundy should be declared a permanent refuge.

Those lucky 200 are the last right whales in the North Atlantic, the few survivors of an earlier quest for oil. It is ironic that again, they are threatened by our need, our greed, for oil.

BIOLOGICAL PROFILE

The **NORTHERN RIGHT WHALE**, *Eubalaena glacialis*, is a baleen whale, Mysticeti, belonging to the family of right whales called Balaenidae. In Quebec, it is called *baleine franche* or *baleine noire*.

Size

Northern right whales measure 35 to 50 feet long — 60 feet for the largest females — and may weigh up to 100 tons. Calves are 15 to 20 feet at birth.

Features

Right whales have a large, stocky body (the girth can be 60 percent or more of body length) that tapers to a narrow tail, large spatulate flippers, a smooth back without a dorsal fin and no ventral grooves. The huge head (about one-quarter of total body length) features a bowed lower jaw that enfolds the long, narrow, highly arched upper jaw. Callosities — irregular crusty protuberances of horny material called keratin — found in patches on the head, distinguish right whales from all other whales. The largest callosity, called the bonnet, is located in front of the two blowholes. Colouring: black, though sometimes mottled, with white patches on throat and belly; because of infestations of whale lice (cyamid crustaceans), the callosities may appear white, orange, yellowish or pink. The right whale's V-shaped blow is bushy and often about 15 feet high. Rights have 206 to 268 narrow, dark baleen plates, each up to 8 feet long, on both sides of the mouth. The baleen is fringed with long, fine greyish bristles.

Diet

Right whales are specialized eaters, preferring copepods (tiny planktonic crustaceans) and then euphausiids (krill). They feed near the surface.

Natural History

Males probably become sexually mature at 47½ to 51 feet, females at 49 to 52½ feet, or at about the age of 10. Cows calve in winter or spring every 2 to 4 years (usually 3, based on studies of the southern right whale) after a 12-month gestation. However, studies in the lower Bay of Fundy suggest that some conceptions may occur in August or September. Calves, born with no callosities, nurse for 1 to 2 years, and there is a strong cow/calf bond. On the winter breeding grounds, cows and their calves are segregated from mating whales. Several males may court a single female at the same time. There is a seasonal north-south migration, but migrating right whales may stay in one area for weeks. Right whales rarely dive deep and usually remain underwater for only about 20 minutes. They can be very acrobatic, breaching and smacking the surface with their tails (lobtailing) or flippers (flippering). Their vocalizations are expressive low-frequency moans and belchlike utterances. Right whales are slow swimmers and are generally docile and easy to approach — traits that whalers exploited. They are preyed upon by killer whales.

Attacking a right whale. Lithograph by Currier & Ives.

Range

Right whales once ranged throughout the cooler waters of the northern hemisphere but exist today only in remnant populations, the best known of which is in the lower Bay of Fundy. They can be found near shore in shallow water or in large bays. They have been observed in the Gulf of St. Lawrence and off the coasts of Nova Scotia, Newfoundland and Labrador.

Status

Nearly extinct since the 1920s, right whales are fully protected. Heavy whaling pared their numbers to the current estimates of 220 individuals in the North Pacific and 200 in the North Atlantic. In earlier centuries, hundreds of right whales could be observed on feeding grounds, but today, only a few at a time can be seen.

Whaling operations. Engraving, 1768.

C-103905 Public Archives Canada

Sperm Whale

The Generic Whale

Moby-Dick, the star of Melville's classic novel, was a sperm whale. A big, old male, he was portrayed as cantankerous and malevolent — able, even eager, to smash a sailing ship to splinters. Perhaps Captain Ahab just brought out the worst in him.

Sperm whale researcher Hal Whitehead of the Memorial University of Newfoundland, who has spent most of the last several years watching sperm whales, found them almost shy. When divers slipped into the water to film the mixed groups of females, calves and young males, the sperms turned their great black heads away from the camera and defecated nervously as they swam out of range.

Whitehead served his whale apprenticeship in the North Atlantic, photographing the tails of humpback whales around Newfoundland and on the Grand Banks. But to study sperm whales — which, although present, are far offshore on Canadian coasts — he had to go to Sri Lanka.

The possibility of finding and studying sperm whales was actually remote when Whitehead joined a sailing expedition to survey the Indian Ocean in 1982. Only a few years earlier, the International Whaling Commission had designated the Indian Ocean as a whale sanctuary. In an effort to find out what whale life existed there, the World Wildlife Fund of the Netherlands sponsored a three-year survey. Together with whale researchers Abigail Alling, Jonathan Gordon

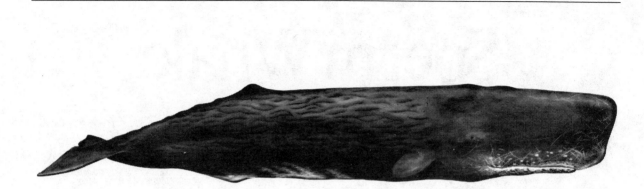

SPERM WHALE

Physeter macrocephalus

and others, Whitehead sailed through the Red Sea and across the Indian Ocean. They spoke with fishermen, biologists and government representatives, and they photographed and recorded every whale and dolphin they could get close to. The surprise came in the second season when they discovered that large numbers of sperm and blue whales were accessible for study near Sri Lanka.

The biology of the sperm whale is well known to science. As the longtime mainstay of the whaling industry, the sperm whale in its every part has been measured, weighed and duly noted, and the basic reproductive data have been established. Yet few scientists have looked at the living animal. One factor that has impeded study is the sperm's ability to hold its breath. Feeding at great depths on squid, a sperm routinely remains underwater for an hour at a time, and 1½-hour dives have been recorded. When a sperm surfaces, it takes many short breaths — the old whaler's rule of thumb, probably somewhat exaggerated, was one breath per minute down — and then disappears for another hour. Coming up next time, it might be miles away.

To find and track sperm whales, Whitehead and his colleagues lowered a directional hydrophone, or underwater microphone, in the ocean and followed the steady rhythmic clicks emitted by the sperm whales — probably used mainly to locate food. The clicks can be heard up to three or four miles away, depending on sea conditions and the depth of the whales. Typically, the whales began clicking at 650 to 1,000 feet. The deepest clicks were recorded at 3,000 feet — the limit of the ship's depth sounder — but Whitehead is certain that they sometimes dive deeper.

When a young calf and one or more adults were at the surface, they stayed directly above those diving below. At these times, Whitehead and his colleagues took advantage of the photographic opportunities and got their IDs, focusing on the nicks, scratches and minor injuries on dorsal humps, backs and tail flukes.

For 3½ days, they followed one group of 13 sperm whales, watching a young calf swim beside three different adults within a 90-minute period. With most whales and dolphins, the adult animal accompanying a young calf is usually its mother, but not with sperm whales. Unable to hold its breath for long periods, the calf waits at or near the surface, attended by an adult baby-sitter. The baby-sitting chore is shared by the adults, apparently giving each a chance to dive deep and feed.

In some ways, sperm whales are the most familiar of all whales. It is this species' image that is the generic whale — inspiring everything from brass door knockers to bathtub toys. But in other ways, sperm whales are the most mysterious. This largest species of toothed whale has the biggest brain of any creature on Earth — at 17 pounds, almost six times the size of a human brain.

What could it be used for?

Unravelling the full story of the sperm whale is a supreme challenge for man, struggling with that comparatively minuscule tool: the three-pound human brain.

BIOLOGICAL PROFILE

The **SPERM WHALE**, *Physeter macrocephalus*, is a toothed whale, Odontoceti, belonging to the family of sperm whales called Physeteridae. It is known as *cachalot* or *cachalot macrocéphale* in Quebec.

Size

Male sperm whales may reach almost 60 feet in length and weigh 58 tons but are usually about 50 feet, while females measure less than 37 feet. Newborn sperms are 11½ to 15 feet long and weigh about a ton.

Features

Sperm whales are massive, with a large squarish head (one-third to one-quarter total body length) and a low humplike dorsal fin set two-thirds of the way back from the tip of the snout. They have prunelike skin, bumps, or knuckles, along the back from the dorsal fin to the broad triangular tail flukes and short, stubby flippers. The dorsal fin and the bumpy ridge are visible when the animal begins to dive. The sperm whale's blunt snout, squarish in profile, projects up to 5 feet beyond the lower jaw and contains spermaceti, a high-quality oil. Colouring: dark brown to dark grey, with light grey or white areas around the belly, the forehead and the corners of the mouth; calves are light tan or grey overall. The single S-shaped blowhole sits so far to the left that the sperm whale's blow easily identifies the species. The bushy spout, less than 10 feet high, has a pronounced forward cant — more like the angle of cannon fire than most whales' tall plumes. Sperms have 18 to 25 teeth on each side of the narrow lower jaw; tooth sockets and unerupted rudimentary teeth are present in the upper jaw.

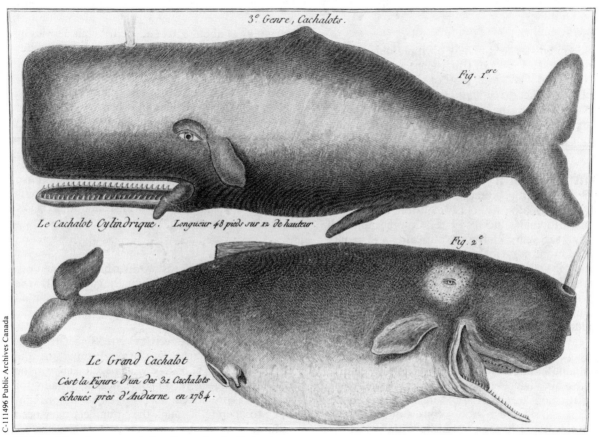

3.º Genre, Cachalots.

Fig. 1.ᵉʳᵉ

Le Cachalot Cylindrique. Longueur 48 pieds sur 12 de hauteur

Fig. 2.ᵉ

Le Grand Cachalot

C'est la Figure d'un des 31 Cachalots
échoués près d'Audierne en 1784.

Male and female sperm whales. Engraving by Benard.

Diet

Sperm whales feed mainly on squid but also eat octopus and a variety of fish, such as salmon, rockfish, lingcod and skates, most of which live at great depths (1,500 feet to perhaps 2 miles). They sometimes gather food along the sea bottom. On an average day, a large male sperm eats about 3.5 percent of its body weight in squid.

Natural History

Sexual maturity is reached between 8 and 11 years of age for females, at about 27 to 30 feet, and 10 years or more for males, at 33 to 39 feet. Cows bear one calf every 4 to 5 years. Calves are born after a 15-month gestation and nurse for approximately 2 years. Unable to remain underwater for long periods, the calves hang near the surface, attended by an adult. The baby-sitting chore is shared, allowing all members of the group an opportunity to feed. During migration, males range farther north and south than females and juveniles. Older males travel alone or in small groups, except during the breeding season. The prevalence of tooth marks on the skin of most males suggests that large males fight over females. Sperm whale groups of 50 or more are common and are usually segregated by age and sex. Such groups consist of sexually inactive males, juveniles, and females with their calves.

Beginning at about 650 feet, sperms emit a series of steady rhythmic clicks that can be heard up to 4 miles away. These clicks, which have been recorded at depths of 3,000 feet, are probably used to locate food. After a deep dive, sperm whales may remain on the surface for at least an hour, blowing 50 times or more before the next dive. Sperm whales have up to 17-pound brains, the largest of any creature on Earth. Besides the valuable oil stored in their snouts, sperm whales produce ambergris, which is still sometimes used as a perfume fixative, though synthetics have proved a popular substitute. Lumps of ambergris weighing up to 225 pounds form around squid beaks in the lower intestine.

Range

Sperm whales are widely distributed in the deep waters of the world ocean, from the equatorial to the polar seas.

Status

Sperm whales have been harvested since the beginning of the 18th century. Current estimates of the population are 732,000, of which 322,000 live in the northern hemisphere. In 1979, oceanic whaling of sperms was prohibited, but shore-based stations continue to operate. Though their numbers have been reduced, they are not endangered.

Cuvier's Beaked Whale

Elusive Warrior

In 1823, a skull found on a beach west of Marseilles inspired the French naturalist Baron Georges Cuvier to describe the species that has come to bear his name. Since then, many more skulls and carcasses of stranded Cuvier's beaked whales have been collected around the world, adding to our knowledge about the species. But accounts of their living behaviour are rare. A few reports from whalers are all we have.

Cuvier's beaked whales are sometimes caught in the seagoing Japanese fishery that hunts small whales and harvests everything it catches. The whalers don't go out looking for a Cuvier and expect to find one. But when they do, it is usually in waters deeper than 3,000 feet. Typically, the Cuviers are seen in groups of 10 to 20, and when pursued, they all submerge at once. A Cuvier often raises its flukes straight out of the water and descends vertically, staying down for at least 30 minutes.

Like most other beaked whales, the look of the male differs from the female. The teeth in a female Cuvier do not erupt; in males, a single nonfunctioning pair of teeth protrudes from the tip of the lower jaw.

Many beaked whales, particularly the older males, are heavily scarred, their bodies crisscrossed with teeth marks. Until whale researchers develop ways of finding and studying beaked whales in the wild, we can only imagine the great battles — or boisterous play — that must occur between males half a mile or more

CUVIER'S BEAKED WHALE

Ziphius cavirostris

below the surface of the sea.

BIOLOGICAL PROFILE

The CUVIER'S BEAKED WHALE, *Ziphius cavirostris*, is a toothed whale, Odontoceti, belonging to the family of beaked whales called Ziphiidae. It is sometimes called the goose-beaked whale or, in Quebec, *ziphius de Cuvier*.

Size

Male Cuvier's beaked whales measure 18 to 22 feet long, females 19 to 23 feet. Calves are 6½ to 10 feet at birth.

Features

Cuvier's beaked whales are robust and have a small head with a gradually sloping forehead and a relatively short beak. Their curved or triangular dorsal fin is up to 15 inches high and set well back. Like other beaked whales, they have tiny flippers and a pair of V-shaped throat grooves. The lower jaw protrudes beyond the upper jaw. In profile, the head and mouth line resemble a goose beak. Colouring: tan to light brown; belly usually lighter and covered with white or cream-coloured oval blotches; heavily scarred body is often purplish or reddish in sunlight; lighter head in older individuals, turning almost white in males. A Cuvier's

blow is low and inconspicuous, angled slightly forward and to the left. Conical teeth erupt only in males — one on each side near the tip of the lower jaw. They are exposed and often quite worn.

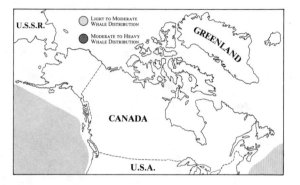

Diet

Cuvier's beaked whales consume squid and deep-water fish.

Range

Cuvier's beaked whales are widely distributed in the offshore tropical and temperate waters of the world ocean. Although they range far from continental landmasses, they strand (sometimes alive) more often than any other beaked whale.

Natural History

Sexual maturity is reached when females are about 19½ feet and males 18 feet. Apparently wary of boats, Cuviers are rarely observed at sea, and details of their natural history are little known. Occasionally, bulls travel alone. Cuviers are vigorous swimmers, appearing and disappearing suddenly. When pursued, they all submerge at once. They take only a short rest at the surface before diving again and stay down for at least 30 minutes. They have been known to breach and often raise their flukes vertically before beginning a deep dive.

Status

Unknown.

The whale fishery. Woodcut.

Northern Bottlenose Whale

The Flathead

There are about 18 known species belonging to the family of beaked whales, and at least 11 of them might technically be found in Canadian waters. But only one — the northern bottlenose whale — is encountered regularly.

Two areas with year-round concentrations are the northern Labrador Sea, near the entrance to Hudson Strait, and the Gully, southeast of Nova Scotia, near Sable Island. Only the more adventurous whale researchers have visited the bottlenose in these deep-sea regions.

Most beaked whales are shy, but not the northern bottlenose. Unlike the others, the northern bottlenose readily approaches ships, a trait that made it popular with whalers. From the late 19th century until the 1960s, whalers from Norway (and, to a lesser extent, from Scotland and Canada) hunted northern bottlenose, killing up to a few thousand a year, mostly for oil and animal food. The species seems to have been depleted, at least in the eastern North Atlantic.

Northern bottlenose whales are tremendous divers — among the greatest of all whales and dolphins. Harpooned northern bottlenoses have been known to dive straight down, taking out 500 fathoms (3,000 feet) of line in 2 minutes. Undisturbed bottlenoses may stay down for 14 to 70 minutes. Northern bottlenoses prefer deep-water habitats, 3,000 feet or more, where they feed on squid. One captured bottlenose reportedly

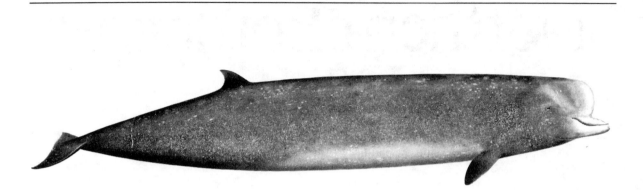

NORTHERN BOTTLENOSE WHALE

Hyperoodon ampullatus

had more than 10,000 squid beaks in its multichambered stomach, while other stomachs have contained such bottom-dwelling delicacies as starfish and sea cucumbers.

BIOLOGICAL PROFILE

The **NORTHERN BOTTLENOSE WHALE**, *Hyperoodon ampullatus*, is a toothed whale, Odontoceti, belonging to the family of beaked whales called Ziphiidae. Whalers sometimes referred to this whale as a flathead or bottlehead. In French, it is called *baleine à bec commune*.

Size
Northern bottlenose females measure up to 26 feet long, males up to 32 feet; they can weigh several tons. Calves are about 11 feet at birth.

Features
Northern bottlenose whales have a long, round body, an extremely bulbous forehead, a large dolphin-like beak, a pair of short V-shaped throat grooves, broad flukes and a small, curved dorsal fin at least a foot high and located two-thirds of the way back from the head. Colouring: brown or grey, fading to white or yellow (particularly on the head) in older males; often lighter below; calves are uniformly chocolate

brown. From a crescent-shaped blowhole, located in an indented area behind the forehead, comes a bushy 6-foot-high spout that angles slightly forward. Conical teeth erupt only in males — one on each side near the tip of the lower jaw. Rarely, a series of toothpick-sized teeth are present in the lower jaw.

Diet
Northern bottlenose whales mainly dine on squid, but they also eat herring, starfish, sea cucumbers and other bottom invertebrates.

Natural History
Northern bottlenose whales reach sexual maturity at 22½ to 24½ feet on average. Females are then about 11 years old, males 7 to 11 years. Gestation lasts

75

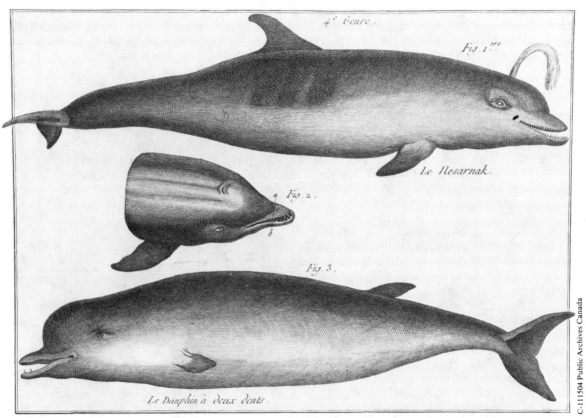

4ᵉ *Genre.*

*Fig. 1.*ᵉʳᵉ

Le Nesarnak.

a Fig. 2.
b

Fig. 3.

Le Dauphin à deux dents.

C-111504 Public Archives Canada

Bottlenose dolphin (top and centre) and northern bottlenose whale (bottom). Engraving by Benard.

about 12 months. Cows give birth every 2 to 3 years, and calves nurse for at least a year. The peak breeding and calving season is spring. Bottlenose whales appear to follow a regular migratory pattern. They summer in sub-Arctic and Arctic waters and begin to move southward in late summer. Some may winter along the edge of the pack ice. Bottlenose whales frequently travel in groups of 5 to 15, but pairs and singles are also seen. There is some seasonal segregation by sex, although large dominant males may travel with groups of females and calves. Like many other whales and dolphins, bottlenose whales have strong social ties and will not abandon an injured companion until it is dead. A young male and female that stranded at Beverly Farms, Massachusetts, in the 1920s reportedly emitted deep groaning and sobbing sounds that could be heard half a mile away. Northern bottlenose whales are among the greatest divers of all whales and dolphins. They can dive 3,000 feet straight down in 2 minutes and may stay submerged for 14 to 70 minutes. Between dives, they blow at the surface for about 10 minutes. They have been observed breaching and smacking the surface with their tails (lobtailing). Bot-tlenose whales eagerly approach ships — a fatal characteristic that made them popular with whalers. They may be preyed upon by killer whales.

Range

Northern bottlenose whales prefer the deep waters of the North Atlantic, especially the cooler waters of the Arctic. Some have even been observed in the broken pack ice. There are year-round concentrations in the northern Labrador Sea, near the entrance to Hudson Strait, and the Gully, southeast of Nova Scotia, near Sable Island. They sometimes visit deep channels in the Gulf of St. Lawrence and the bays and fiords off eastern Newfoundland.

Status

Current numbers are unknown, but the population was apparently reduced substantially by intensive whaling from the late 19th century to the late 1960s. Presently, there is no large-scale hunting of northern bottlenose whales.

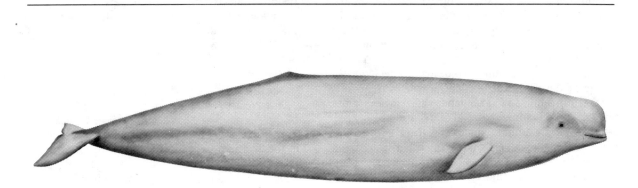

BELUGA

Delphinapterus leucas

Beluga

Ghostly Screamer

The beluga, or white whale, moves like a friendly spectre through the often icy, treacherous northern seas. In the Arctic summer, belugas convene by the hundreds, the pregnant cows to give birth in warm, shallow waters and all of them to feed in the rivers. The shores of the Churchill River of northern Manitoba and the confluence of the St. Lawrence and Saguenay Rivers of Quebec are two of the most accessible land spots from which to watch belugas. Lone belugas have ventured 600 miles up the Yukon River and more than 1,000 miles up the Amur River in Russia. In 1966, one adventurous beluga paddled up the Rhine River into the heart of Germany, drawing screaming crowds wherever it went. The beluga screamed right back.

In Russia's vast northland, a noisy neighbour is said to be "screaming like a beluga." Early whalers who heard the sounds of belugas through the hulls of their ships called them sea canaries. In 1949, U.S. biologists William E. Schevill and Barbara Lawrence visited Quebec, suspending a hydrophone in waters near the mouth of the Saguenay River..They found that belugas had one of the most varied vocal repertoires of any whale and compared them in loquaciousness to such "chatterboxes" as monkeys and humans.

According to Schevill and Lawrence, beluga sounds are "high-pitched resonant whistles and squeals, varied with ticking and clucking sounds — slightly reminiscent of a string orchestra tuning up — as well as mewing and occasional chirps. Sometimes, the calls would suggest a crowd of children shouting in the distance. At other times, there were sharp reports, somewhat like a blow with a split bat or a slap on the water."

As with every toothed whale, the beluga produces sounds in the air passages of its head, apparently directing them through the melon, or forehead. It hears sounds mainly by bone conduction through the mandible, or jaw. But the beluga may also orient to sound by turning its head from side to side. Like the narwhal, the beluga's seven-vertebrae neck is not fused, allowing considerable head mobility. The beluga can dramatically alter the shape of the melon, making it bulge or collapse — apparently at will — to aid in sending or receiving different kinds of sounds.

What little we know about belugas comes mostly from their aquarium life. As early as 1877, a beluga captured in Labrador was shipped to the Westminster Aquarium in London, England. Having survived several weeks in transit, it died only two days after arrival. Other attempts were made in the late 19th and early 20th century with limited success. In 1961, Carleton Ray's expedition to Alaska captured three juvenile belugas for the New York Aquarium, one of which is still alive. Most of the belugas captured for world aquariums since the mid-1960s have come from Churchill, Manitoba, on Hudson Bay.

Why are belugas white?

Comparing belugas to certain Arctic land animals, the white could be camouflage. But the white would not prove an adequate cover at sea, where their bodies gleam like beacons in the dark water. Beluga calves are born a dark shade of grey or even brown and lighten only gradually over the first 5 or 6 years. Perhaps the *dark* colours provide better camouflage, and the calves — the least able to deal with predators — get the advantage.

Beluga predators include killer whales, polar bears and perhaps the odd walrus, but camouflage is irrelevant to a predator like the killer whale, which can use sonar to track its prey.

David E. Sergeant, a Department of Fisheries and Oceans biologist at the Arctic Biological Station in Quebec, has studied belugas in Hudson Bay and in the St. Lawrence. The St. Lawrence belugas were thought to be on their way out, reduced in number and range and affected by high PCB and mercury levels. Researcher Leone Pippard had sounded the alarm after spending three summers studying belugas in the mid-1970s. Sergeant's 1981-83 research in the St. Lawrence, however, revealed that the birth and survival rate to maturity is similar to Arctic belugas and that the St. Lawrence belugas, estimated to number about 500, are beginning to increase in range and are no longer in trouble.

BIOLOGICAL PROFILE

The **BELUGA**, *Delphinapterus leucas*, is a toothed whale, Odontoceti, belonging to the family of white whales called Monodontidae (the narwhal is the only other living member). It is also known as the white whale and, in Quebec, *béluga* or *marsouin blanc*.

and a narrow bumpy ridge extending along the back from the middle; the body tapers at both ends. Their relatively small head has an enlarged rounded forehead, a short broad beak and a clearly defined flexible neck (the cervical vertebrae are not fused, allowing a beluga to turn and nod its head). Colouring: pure white in adults; calves are dark grey or brown and gradually fade to white around the age of 5 or 6. The beluga's blowhole is a crosswise slit located in front of the neck crease. Up to 11 conical teeth are situated on each side of both jaws, often only 32 in all. The teeth are sometimes curved and considerably worn.

Size

Beluga males measure up to 15 feet long and weigh about 1½ tons; females are slightly smaller. Newborn calves are 4 to 5 feet and weigh 75 to 100 pounds.

Features

Belugas are chubby, with creases and folds of fat. They have upcurled flippers and flukes, no dorsal fin

Diet

Belugas eat a wide variety of fish, crustaceans and cephalopods, such as capelin, char, sand lance, pollack, salmon, several cods, shrimp and octopus.

Range

Belugas are generally found in the shallow coastal waters, rivers and estuaries of the Arctic, but some groups live in the St. Lawrence River and in the North Pacific, off Alaska's south-central coast. Two of the most accessible areas to observe belugas are the Saguenay and St. Lawrence Rivers and the Churchill River in northern Manitoba.

Beluga at Chesterfield, N.W.T., 1926.

Natural History

Females become sexually mature at 4 to 7 years, males at 8 to 9 years. Mating occurs in the spring or early summer. The gestation period is 14 months, and cows give birth every 2 to 3 years. Calves stay with their mothers for 2 years. Some beluga populations are migratory, while others reside in a specific area year-round. They may be found near shore or in deep water. Belugas travel in groups as small as 2 or 3, but large herds numbering more than a thousand form in the summer and swim up the major northern rivers. They have been spotted 600 miles inland in the Yukon River. Belugas are highly social animals, and their vocalizations — frequently audible above the surface — may be the most varied of any whale. They were dubbed sea canaries by early mariners because of their assorted repertoire of sounds. These noises are produced in the air passages in the beluga's head and are then directed through the forehead, which changes shape as the beluga sends and then receives various sounds. They are slow swimmers — less than 6 miles per hour — making them prey for killer whales. They are also hunted by polar bears, which wait for belugas to surface along narrow cracks in the ice and then drag them out of the water. They sometimes suffocate under fast-forming ice or starve when shifting ice entraps them.

Status

The Soviet Union is the only country that still hunts belugas commercially, but native hunting continues throughout much of their circumpolar range. One of the most serious dangers that belugas face comes from human interference with their environment: river dams, man-made islands, pipelines and tanker and icebreaker traffic in polar regions. The total population is estimated at 62,000 to 88,000. Once believed endangered in the St. Lawrence, belugas are now estimated to number 500 there, with normal calf production and survival to maturity.

NARWHAL

Monodon monoceros

Narwhal

Acoustic Jousting

For centuries, when the tusk of the male narwhal washed up on northern European beaches, it was thought to be the horn of the legendary unicorn. Yet as marine zoologists are learning, the true story of the narwhal and its tusk may be even more extraordinary than tales of the unicorn.

The narwhal's tusk is actually a tooth — one of two embedded in the upper jaw. In the male narwhal, it erupts at 12 months of age, piercing the upper lip in a counterclockwise spiral until, at maturity, it can be a 10-foot-long tusk. Normally, it's the left tooth. Rarely, the right one also erupts, though it usually grows only a few feet. There are a few instances of females with tusks and one account, from the 19th century, of a two-tusked female.

Canadian zoologist Robin C. Best has analyzed the existing theories on the purpose of the tusk: Might it serve as a tool to spear fish or to stir up prey resting on the muddy bottom? Might the narwhal use it to open breathing holes in the ice? Could it be a defensive weapon against predators such as the walrus, killer whale or polar bear?

No to all of these theories, says Best. For one thing, the tusk is too fragile for such uses. (According to one study, 30 to 40 percent of adult males break their tusks anyway.) Secondly, if the tusk were of critical survival value, particularly for food shopping, all females would have them too — especially since they often travel separately from males. As for opening holes in the ice, belugas and female narwhals do fine with no tusks.

In the absence of a specific use, Best concludes that the tusk probably serves as a "secondary sex character." Whaler William Scoresby Jr. first proposed this theory in the early 19th century, and author Fred Bruemmer and biologist Arthur M. Mansfield later came to the same conclusion based on their own observations in the 1960s.

A narwhal's tusk may function as a visual indicator of size and age — like the horns of a mountain sheep. The male with the largest "rack" gets the female and the first chance at ensuring that his genes are passed on to the next generation. University of Calgary ethologist Valerius Geist has shown that rival rams compare their respective statuses visually, instead of fighting, and so save their energies. Fighting is necessary only between males with almost equal-sized horns.

Whether narwhals have duels with their tusks is a source of disagreement among biologists, but like other toothed whales, male narwhals do have scars on their bodies, notably their heads. In the wild, they have been observed crossing their tusks at the surface. Best suggests that males of nearly equal status may approach head-on, with the longer-tusked male placing his tusk tip on his opponent's acoustically sensitive lower jaw or on his melon (forehead). The longer tusk

may be sufficient to determine the victor, or, as Best hypothesizes, a kind of acoustic duel may ensue. When a narwhal vocalizes, his tusk vibrates; thus the narwhal with the longer tusk might have the superior acoustic "weapon" and be able to overpower his opponent with sound.

Most of the world's narwhals — some 10,000 to 30,000, according to various estimates — live in the Canadian Arctic. Every spring, narwhals move from their Baffin Bay and Davis Strait wintering grounds to the eastern Canadian high Arctic and northwest Greenland. Summer concentrations occur in such fiords as Admiralty Inlet and Eclipse Sound on northern Baffin Island.

In these waters, over the last decade, narwhal researchers Kerwin J. Finley, Rolph A. Davis, Randall R. Reeves and others have observed the annual narwhal hunt by the Inuit and have expressed concern over the number of animals taken and those that are wasted — killed or wounded, but not landed. Bullet-scarred narwhals number as high as 35 percent in some samples of those whaled around Pond Inlet, Baffin Island. The hunt is regulated by the Canadian government, but in practice, the quotas have often been exceeded. Finley believes in teaching conservation. We must work closely with Inuit hunters, he says, to develop better hunting methods and to help them understand and follow the regulations. It is also essential that we learn more about the narwhals' biology and population dynamics to refine the annual quotas. A positive note is a $2 million 1983-85 research project on Arctic whales sponsored by several Canadian foundations, including the World Wildlife Fund and the federal government through the Department of Fisheries and Oceans.

BIOLOGICAL PROFILE

The **NARWHAL**, *Monodon monoceros*, is a toothed whale, Odontoceti, belonging to the family of white whales called Monodontidae. It is called *tugalik* by the Inuit and *narval* by Quebeckers.

Size

Male narwhals grow up to 16 feet long, not including their tusks, and weigh about 1½ tons; females are a little smaller. Calves are about 5 feet at birth and weigh about 175 pounds.

Range

Narwhals like the deep water of the high Arctic and navigate through pack ice to the edge of the icecap. During the spring breakup, some narwhals enter coastal waters. There are large concentrations in Davis Strait, Baffin Bay and the Greenland Sea. Smaller groups are found in Hudson Strait, northern Hudson Bay, Foxe Basin and the Barents Sea.

Features

Narwhals are cylinder-shaped, with a smooth, finless back, except for a few bumps near the tail. They have upcurled flippers and fan-shaped flukes. Their rather small, rounded head has a bulbous forehead, a narrow mouth and only the hint of a beak. Colouring: newborn calves are a blotchy dark blue or grey; as the animal grows, it turns blackish as a juvenile, and then, near maturity, white streaks and patches appear and spread from the underside to the outer flanks; adults have a mottled or spotted back with a white belly; older animals may be nearly all white. A single crescent-shaped blowhole is located on top of the head

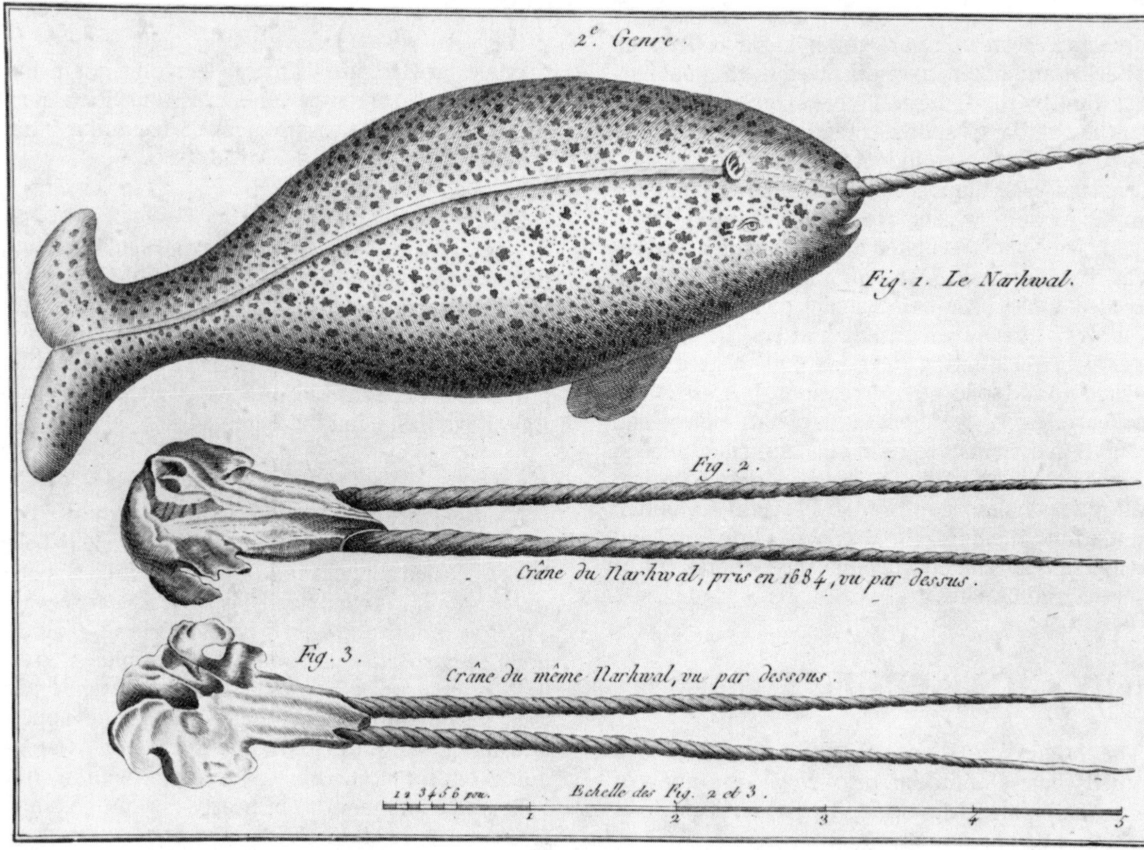

2ᵉ Genre.

Fig. 1. Le Narhwal.

Fig. 2.

Crâne du Narhwal, pris en 1684, vu par dessus.

Fig. 3.

Crâne du même Narhwal, vu par dessous.

1 2 3 4 5 6 pou.   Echelle des Fig. 2 et 3.
    1   2   3   4   5

Figure 1, common narwhal; Figures 2 and 3, rare example of two-tusked narwhal. Engraving by Benard.

to the left of centre. The narwhal has no teeth in its mouth; two adult teeth are embedded in the upper jaw, and the left one, in the male, erupts through the lip at about 12 months of age and grows in a counterclockwise spiral. It can reach 10 feet long at maturity, weigh 22 pounds and measure 8 inches in circumference at the base.

Diet

Narwhals eat squid, Greenland halibut and other bottom fish, as well as polar cod, crabs and shrimp.

Natural History

Females attain sexual maturity at 4 to 7 years of age, males at 8 to 9 years. Mating probably occurs in April, and gestation lasts 14 to 15 months. Calves nurse for at least a year. Cows give birth about every 3 years. The tusk is probably used by males to establish a dominance hierarchy in which physical or social advantage is gained by the bull with the longest tusk. Duels may take place during the breeding season, as evidenced by the scars on the heads of many adult males. Some older males have broken tusks with smoothly polished ends. Narwhal migrations are dictated by advancing and retreating ice. The animals tend to clump in groups throughout their range, and thousands have been observed travelling together. The average size, however, is about 20. Mixed herds are not unusual, but they are often segregated into three groups: juveniles; cows and calves; and tusked bulls. They are sometimes observed close to belugas. A dramatic sight is a male narwhal standing vertically in the water, its head and tusk visible. As Arctic whales, narwhals sometimes become trapped by fast-forming ice. Using their foreheads, they are able to butt breathing holes in ice up to 6 inches thick. Narwhals are occasionally preyed upon by killer whales and only rarely by walruses and polar bears.

Status

Every summer, 20,000 or more narwhals enter Lancaster Sound in the eastern Canadian Arctic. Several thousand may reside in the Soviet Arctic, but few remain in the Beaufort, Bering and eastern Chukchi Seas. The narwhal is hunted in Greenland and Canada primarily for its ivory tusk but also for its blubber.

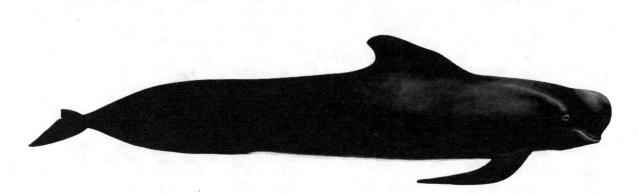

LONG-FINNED PILOT WHALE

Globicephala melaena

Long-finned Pilot Whale

Stranded High and Dry

August 1, 1960: 58 long-finned pilot whales strand at Port Maitland, Nova Scotia. All die.

September 28, 1975: 300 long-finned pilot whales beach themselves at Charleston, Bonavista Bay, Newfoundland. Fishermen are hired to try to return them to the sea.

July 16, 1979: 300 long-finned pilot whales strand near Point au Gaul on the Burin Peninsula, Newfoundland. All die.

Why do these whales beach themselves en masse? No whale is stranded high and dry on Canadian shores as often or in as large numbers as the long-finned pilot whale.

Pilot whales swim chiefly in the deep-sea swells near the edge of the continental shelf. Here, they dine on the abundant squid, their preferred and almost exclusive food. So accomplished are they at tracking and catching squid that other dolphins, birds and even fishermen will let the whales "pilot" them too — not only to squid but also to the herring, mackerel and capelin that the squid feed on. Every year, squid migrate to inshore waters. In the Atlantic Provinces, this happens in summer or early fall. The pilot whales track them in, and then, increasingly in recent years, large groups end up on the beaches. Although no one is certain why this happens, the following theories have been advanced:

• A breakdown of sonar, or echolocation, and therefore an inability to identify the gently sloping beaches they tend to strand on.

• An unfamiliarity with coastal waters, especially those with considerable tidal change.

• Parasites could infest the head and thereby jam sonar reception.

• Simple carelessness amid the frenzy of near-shore feeding.

• Disorientation due to stormy weather with strong onshore winds.

One complicating factor stems from the strong social bonds of pilot whales. Long-finned pilot whale schools contain all sizes of both sexes. Adults are known for their long and unstinting devotion to the young. They will also stick by an injured or endangered comrade. If one pilot whale — perhaps a key individual or leader — became stranded, for whatever reason, it is possible that its distress cries would bring the others to shore too. Researchers finding live whales freshly stranded or in shallow water have towed them out to sea, only to watch as they returned to shore to die. Some researchers believe if they could identify the leader, or distressed animal, and either return it to the sea or, if it was determined to be unhealthy, kill it, perhaps the other animals could be saved.

Department of Fisheries and Oceans biologist David E. Sergeant has thought a great deal about mass strandings. He went to Newfoundland to study long-finned pilot whales in the 1950s, when fishermen were harvesting them by driving them ashore at a rate of about 5,000 a year. There were few unprovoked beachings then, but the mass strandings increased after whaling declined and finally ended in 1972.

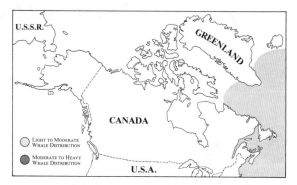

Besides pilot whales, Sergeant has studied the strandings of other species. In a December 1982 paper on mass strandings, Sergeant pointed out that while parasitic disease had been found in singly stranded animals, none has been detected in the mass strandings. He also discounts the theory involving coastline configurations. Analyzing strandings of pilot whales and others, Sergeant concludes that mass strandings of toothed whales occur at points of high population density and especially within the "core" of a species'

range. He suggests that stress could explain the "passive, moribund condition" of animals about to beach themselves and that possible links to stress should be investigated.

In Sergeant's view, mass mortality is a built-in population regulator and the more whales that are "out there," the more strandings. Other researchers are worried about stranded whales and are still trying to figure out how to re-float them, but according to Sergeant, the increase in beachings is really a sign of abundance, of a healthy population.

BIOLOGICAL PROFILE

The **LONG-FINNED PILOT WHALE**, *Globicephala melaena*, is a toothed whale, Odontoceti, belonging to the family of oceanic dolphins called Delphinidae. Newfoundlanders call this whale pothead, and in Quebec, it is called *globicéphale noir*.

Size

Male long-finned pilot whales average 13 feet in length, but can grow to 20 feet, and weigh about 3 tons; females can measure up to 16 feet and weigh 2 to 2½ tons. Newborn calves are about 5½ feet and weigh approximately 175 pounds.

Features

Long-finned pilot whales are robust and have a thick, bulbous head with an upcurved mouth line and just the hint of a beak. They have long sickle-shaped flippers (about one-fifth of body length), a prominent broad-based dorsal fin and a thick keel on the tail. Colouring: black, except for a light anchor-shaped patch on the chest and a pale stripe along the midline of the underside; sometimes a grey saddle behind the dorsal fin in large animals. The crescent-shaped blowhole is located on top of the head just to the left of centre. Pilot whales have 7 to 12 peglike teeth on each side of upper and lower jaws.

Diet

Pilot whales prefer squid, but if squid are unavailable, they will eat cod and other fish. Their daily and seasonal movements are dictated by the migrating squid that they doggedly track.

Natural History

Females reach sexual maturity at approximately 6 years of age; males at about 12. The peak mating season is spring and early summer. Cows give birth every 3 years after a 15-to-16-month gestation. Calves nurse for about 20 months. Pilot whales exhibit strong social bonds. The adults are very devoted to their young and will not desert sick or injured companions. 93

Sperm-whale fishing.

Around Newfoundland, where they have been studied intensively, pilot whales usually arrive inshore in June or July and move to offshore winter grounds in late October or November. Pilot whales stick close together when travelling or being pursued but spread out when feeding. They appear to follow a leader when on the move. Although they generally form groups of about 50, herds of more than a thousand have been reported. Large aggregations appear to contain twice as many cows as bulls. They have been observed in the company of smaller toothed whales, such as bottlenose dolphins. Pilot whales sometimes stand vertically in the water with the head and upper portion of the flippers visible (spyhopping). They have also been seen smacking their tails against the water (lobtailing). They rarely breach and do not ride bow waves. They may live 40 to 50 years. The pilot whale is called pothead because its large bulbous forehead makes it look like it is wearing a pot. Pilot whales have no known predators. Mass strandings can claim up to several hundred animals at a time.

Range

Long-finned pilot whales live in the cool temperate waters of the world ocean, especially near the edge of the continental shelf. Off eastern Canada, they follow the squid, entering inshore waters during the summer.

Status

Long-finned pilot whales have been heavily exploited in the North Atlantic for their meat and oil. The Newfoundland fishery, which supplied food for ranch mink, operated from 1947 to 1972 and seriously depleted the stock off eastern Canada, with annual catches peaking at close to 10,000. Although their current numbers are unknown, pilot whales are believed to be making a comeback.

KILLER WHALE

Orcinus orca

Killer Whale

Ignoring the Rules

When veteran whale researcher Graeme Ellis returned to Nanaimo's Pacific Biological Station following a summer of census work off the northern Vancouver Island coast in 1982, he reported to his boss, marine mammalogist Michael A. Bigg, that there had been no mortalities among the killer whales they had seen in previous summers and that *all* the killer whales were present. The report puzzled Bigg.

After more than a decade of identifying individual killer whales and finding a resident population with stable family units, after monitoring births and deaths all along the British Columbia coast, Bigg and Ellis and associates already knew that the birth and death rates were low — among the lowest of all social mammals. Bigg had begun to calculate a longevity table, and as year after year went by with few, if any, deaths, the statistical ages kept growing.

How can they be living so long? Bigg wondered. It's possible, he admitted, that the last 10 years were especially kind to killer whales — fewer dying — but he didn't think so. Even when he interpreted the rates conservatively, Bigg kept coming up with big age numbers — bulls living for about 50 years, cows topping 100.

Killer whales, the oddballs among social mammals, break all the rules. Bigg and other researchers are discovering some of the behavioural aspects of killers:
Killer whales live in tight inbred associations called

pods. With social mammals such as lions, a male and a female come from different origins to form a mated pair. In time, however, lion families disintegrate and the offspring mix with other lions, forming new bonds. But with killer whale pods, Bigg has found that the only way an individual arrives or leaves is through birth or death. He knows of no case of pod switching. "It's possible that whales may mate outside their pods," says Bigg, "but I don't think so. The killer whales on the B.C. coast must be highly inbred."

Killer whale pods are matriarchal. Bigg talks about calves he photographed 12 years ago that have grown into mature bulls, their dorsal fins shooting up to the characteristic five-foot male size: "And they're still travelling with their mothers!" Bigg has divided every pod into subgroups, which are like cliques within the pod. Each subgroup has one mature cow and progeny of all ages. A few subgroups have no mature cows, "most likely because their mothers have died," says Bigg, for he feels that the cow is the key to understanding the pod and that a productive cow may be the central individual around which new pods form.

Killer whale pods change slowly. With low birth and mortality rates, plus the 100-year life span of a cow, the development of new pods could take hundreds of years. Bigg says that basic change in pod structure may occur only when a pod becomes large enough to split or small enough to die out.

The legendary "killer" is a hard-luck transient. Bigg thinks that pods of fewer than 6 whales are probably doomed to die out. There are 30 pods totalling 261 killer whales living around Vancouver Island, and 50 of them are in 15 pods of fewer than 6 whales. These

small pods are the transients. While the larger resident pods grow fat following the salmon runs around the inshore waters of Vancouver Island, the transients' range extends far offshore; transients may traverse the entire coast, from Alaska to Washington. Consigned to less productive feeding areas, these transients are the famous killer whales of legend — those that will attack seals and occasionally some other whales. And so we discover that the legendary killer is really the hard-luck orca, its alleged fierceness more hunger and desperation than viciousness.

Every killer whale pod has its own dialect. My first work with whales was recording killer whale sounds using hydrophones (underwater microphones) off northern Vancouver Island. Loud enough to carry 7 to 10 miles underwater, the whales' repetitive calls and long, piercing sequences were awe-inspiring. In August 1973, I moved my equipment from northern Vancouver Island to Pedder Bay, where killer whales living off southern Vancouver Island were penned up — recently captured and ready to be shipped to an aquarium. Pedder Bay is only 250 miles south by water, but the captured pod sounded totally different from any I had heard — like another species.

In 1978, John K.B. Ford began a five-year study of killer whale sounds. Using Bigg's "fin prints" of B.C. killer whales, Ford and his wife, Deborah, travelled up and down the coast recording all the pods. They discovered that each pod had at least a few of its own sounds: a dialect. The number of pod-shared sounds usually varied according to how often the whales travelled together in superpods, and pods living close to each other tended to share more sounds. The Fords' work explained what I had heard and found confusing in 1973: northern and southern Vancouver Island killer whale pods never travel together and sound totally different.

In the winter of 1983-84, Ford began installing permanent hydrophones in certain strategic locales along the B.C. coast. The hydrophones are kept underwater year-round, with the signal going to a nearby lighthouse keeper or coastal resident. Jim Borrowman and Bill Mackay of Telegraph Cove, British Columbia, have their living room loudspeakers tuned to Ford's hydrophones in Johnstone Strait. They hear the whales passing by day and by night, through winter storms or summer fogs. If Borrowman and Mackay are unable to identify the pod dialect, they can call Ford in Vancouver and let him listen on the telephone, live. He knows the dialects by heart. Ford, currently writing his doctoral thesis on killer whale dialects at the University of British Columbia in Vancouver, keeps track of killer whales hundreds of miles away, monitoring their dialects.

Only a few other species — *Homo sapiens* included — have true local dialects.

BIOLOGICAL PROFILE

The **KILLER WHALE**, *Orcinus orca*, is a toothed whale, Odontoceti, belonging to the family of toothed whales called Delphinidae. Commonly called orca, the killer whale is known as blackfish on the B.C. coast and *épaulard* in Quebec. Elsewhere, it is sometimes referred to simply as killer.

Size

Male killer whales grow up to 25 feet long (the record is 32 feet) and weigh up to 6 tons; females reach up to 21 feet and about 4 tons. Calves are approximately 7 feet and 450 pounds at birth.

Features

Killer whales are robust and have a conical head with a small or indistinct beak and a straight mouth line. They have large paddle-shaped flippers and a tall dorsal fin (curved in females and immature males; straight and up to 6 feet tall in mature males). Colouring: glossy black, except for greyish saddle patch and striking white belly, flank and eye patches, located above and behind each eye; the eye patches and belly of newborn calves are tannish orange or pink for the first few months. Killer whales have 10 to 13 large conical teeth on each side of both jaws.

Natural History

Males mature at about 19 to 22 feet and females at approximately 16 feet, when they are at least 10 years old. Calves are born after about a 16-month gestation, then nurse for 1 to 2 years. According to B.C. studies, cows give birth every 10 years on average, but some have been known to calve at 3-year intervals. Killer whales exhibit strong social bonds and stable group structure. They belong to pods, which may range from 1 to 50 but usually number about 10. Most pods contain adults of both sexes as well as juveniles and calves. Frequently, several pods travel together in a superpod of a hundred or more. Their movements depend on the availability of food. Each pod has its own dialect, and pods in close proximity to each other often share some sounds. In much of their Northwest Coast range, killer whale pods are resident year-round. However, transients may travel the entire west coast from Alaska to Washington. Killer whales frequently breach, and in order to clear the water at such times, they must reach exit speeds of 22 miles per hour. Their top speed is close to 30 miles per hour.

Diet

Killer whales are famous for their extensive diet; few marine organisms of any size are safe. They devour at least 25 whale and dolphin species, seals, sea lions, squid, birds and even one species of sea turtle, but fish such as salmon, cod and herring are the most common known food items in Canadian waters.

Range

A cosmopolitan species, killer whales are found in all three of Canada's oceans but are most common off the B.C. coast around Vancouver Island. Although they inhabit Canadian waters year-round, summer is the best time to see them.

4.ᵉ *Genre*.

Fig. 1.ᵉʳᵉ

l'Épaulard.

Fig. 2.

L'Épaulard ventru.

Male and female killer whales. Engraving by Benard.

Status

Killer whales have been taken sporadically by many of the world's small-whale fisheries, particularly off Japan and Norway and in the Antarctic. They have also been killed as a control measure in some areas such as Iceland because of their alleged depredation of herring. The world population is unknown, but killer whales do not appear to be endangered. There are 261 killer whales known to inhabit the waters off the B.C. coast.

White-beaked Dolphin

The Squidhound

The white-beaked dolphin got its name in the eastern North Atlantic. In the western North Atlantic, its beak is sometimes speckled or even grey, like that of the Atlantic white-sided dolphin, its close relative. The two species are about the same size, which further confuses positive identification, and they have somewhat overlapping ranges, though the white-beaked appears to prefer cooler waters. The white-beaked dolphin is every bit as active and playful as the Atlantic white-sided. The best way to distinguish the two species is to look closely at the backside. The white-beaked has a patch of white on its backside, while the Atlantic white-sided dolphin has a black back and a tan-yellow rear flank patch.

Greenlanders still occasionally hunt the white-beaked dolphin for food. Norwegians, Icelanders, Scots and Irish, as well as Newfoundlanders, took them in earlier years. Today, like other whales and dolphins, white-beaked dolphins are protected in Canadian waters, though not always welcomed by Newfoundland fishermen. White-beaked dolphins eat cod, capelin, even crustaceans, but it is their squid consumption that irritates the fishermen.

Researchers Abigail Alling, who has worked with dolphins off Newfoundland, and Richard Sears, who studies blue whales in the Gulf of St. Lawrence, have spent time with the white-beaked dolphin, but basic data on this dolphin's life history, including reproduc-

WHITE-BEAKED DOLPHIN

Lagenorhynchus albirostris

tion, are still unknown. From May to November, white-beaked dolphins concentrate around Newfoundland and Labrador as well as in the Gulf of St. Lawrence. They usually travel in herds of 10 to 20, but groups of up to 1,500 have been observed.

BIOLOGICAL PROFILE

The **WHITE-BEAKED DOLPHIN**, *Lagenorhynchus albirostris*, is a toothed whale, Odontoceti, belonging to the family of oceanic dolphins called Delphinidae. Sometimes called lag, the white-beaked dolphin is known as squidhound in Newfoundland and, in Quebec, as *dauphin à nez blanc*, *sauteur* or *cochon de mer*.

Size

White-beaked dolphins measure up to about 10 feet long. Newborn calves are approximately 4 feet.

Features

White-beaked dolphins are robust and have a thick rounded beak, a tall curved dorsal fin, sharp pointed flippers and a gently tapering tail. Colouring: black back with white beak (beak may be speckled or grey in the western North Atlantic), white area on sides extending up to greyish saddle patch that looks white

from a distance and white belly. They have 22 to 28 small teeth on each side of both jaws.

Diet

White-beaked dolphins eat squid, capelin, cod, octopus, herring, haddock and crustaceans.

Natural History

Little is known about their reproductive cycles, but it is believed that gestation lasts about 1 year. Mating probably occurs during the warmer months, with the calves being born between June and September. The movements of white-beaked dolphins are poorly understood. They are found near the northern limits of their range between spring and late autumn and apparently winter to the south. They generally travel in groups of 10 to 20, but herds of up to 1,500 have been observed off Newfoundland and in the Gulf of St. Lawrence. White-beaked dolphins are very acrobatic, often breaching and jumping upside down out of the water. There are no known predators. Single strandings of old individuals are not uncommon.

Range

They are found offshore in the North Atlantic, in cold temperate and sub-Arctic waters. They are abundant from May to November off Newfoundland and Labrador, in the Gulf of St. Lawrence and throughout Davis Strait.

Status

White-beaked dolphin numbers are unknown, but the species is probably not endangered. There are no records of any large-scale hunting of white-beaked dolphins. Some are accidentally killed when they become entangled in trawl nets.

Atlantic White-sided Dolphin

Water Ballet in the North Atlantic

Leaping, spinning and lobtailing, flashing white and tan-yellow sides as it dances through the waves, the Atlantic white-sided dolphin is perhaps the best water show on the open North Atlantic. And white-sided dolphins are sociable. Swimming in schools of 50 to 500 or more, they'll ride the bow wave of a boat, even coast along on the "bow" of a humpback or fin whale, tucking themselves into the pressure wave to hitch a free ride.

Humpback, blue and fin whale researchers often encounter Atlantic white-sided dolphins off the coast of eastern Canada and the United States and in the St. Lawrence, yet most of what we know about the biology of the species has come from two mass strandings:

• On May 15, 1973, about 20 dolphins died on the beach at Cape Cod, near Wellfleet, Massachusetts.
• On September 6, 1974, about 150 dolphins beached themselves in Cobscook Bay, Maine, and 59 of them were trucked to the New England Aquarium for further study.

Department of Fisheries and Oceans biologist David E. Sergeant from Quebec and several Canadian and U.S. colleagues examined the specimens in detail and wrote up their findings. The males, sexually mature at 4 to 6 years, had reached about 7½ feet in length; the females matured at 5 to 8 years of age. By ageing 15 suckling calves, it was determined that mating occurred during July and August and that the

ATLANTIC WHITE-SIDED DOLPHIN

Lagenorhynchus acutus

calves nursed for about 18 months.

No subadult dolphins were present in the two herds, leading Sergeant and his colleagues to conclude that soon after being weaned, the subadults either left or were driven out of the reproductive herd.

Do these subadults remain alone, or do they join others like themselves to form loose groupings?

Most of the single strandings of Atlantic white-sided dolphins have been subadults. According to Sergeant, some subadult loners may join up with pilot whales or even fin and humpback whales to hunt together or just for the company.

BIOLOGICAL PROFILE

The **ATLANTIC WHITE-SIDED DOLPHIN**, *Lagenorhynchus acutus*, is a toothed whale, Odontoceti, belonging to the family of oceanic dolphins called Delphinidae. Newfoundlanders call this dolphin jumper, and Quebeckers call it *dauphin à flancs blancs*, *sauteur* or *cochon de mer*. Elsewhere in Canada, it is sometimes called lag.

Size

Atlantic white-sided dolphins measure 6½ to 9 feet long and can weigh more than 500 pounds; the females are slightly smaller than the males. Newborn calves are about 4 feet.

Features

Atlantic white-sided dolphins are somewhat robust with a sharply pointed dorsal fin, sickle-shaped flippers and an extremely thick tail stock. The forehead slopes gradually toward the short, thick bicoloured beak. Colouring: black back, including tail, flippers and top of beak; white belly and underside of beak; a black eye patch; and a greyish flank with a narrow, white streak connected to diagnostic tan or yellow patch at rear; a thin dark stripe also runs from corner of mouth to flipper. They have 30 to 40 small, pointed teeth on each side of both jaws.

U.S.S.R.
GREENLAND
CANADA

○ LIGHT TO MODERATE WHALE DISTRIBUTION
● MODERATE TO HEAVY WHALE DISTRIBUTION

U.S.A.

Diet

Atlantic white-sided dolphins feed on squid and herring as well as smelt, silver hake and shrimp.

Natural History

Females reach sexual maturity at 5 to 8 years, males at 4 to 6 years (when they are approximately 7½ feet long). Calves are born in June and July after an 11-month gestation and nurse for about 18 months. Mating occurs during July and August, and cows probably give birth every 2 to 3 years. Small groups of 6 or 8 Atlantic white-sided dolphins are observed in inshore areas during the summer, while offshore herds may number many hundreds. There is evidence of some segregation: immature and newly matured animals are not present in breeding groups. Atlantic white-sided dolphins are very sociable animals and are frequently found in the company of long-finned pilot whales and humpback whales. It is believed that they communicate with each other through a series of barks, groans, chirps and whistles as well as with their body posture and by slapping their flukes on the surface. They are fast swimmers and very visible at sea. Although they are wary of ships, they occasionally ride the bow waves. Atlantic white-sided dolphins are sometimes preyed upon by sharks and killer whales, and individual and mass strandings are common.

Range

Atlantic white-sided dolphins inhabit the cooler temperate offshore waters of the North Atlantic. They are common around Newfoundland and Labrador and range into the St. Lawrence and the Bay of Fundy.

Status

Their total numbers are unknown, but the western North Atlantic population is estimated at 24,000. For years, they were killed in the hundreds, along with pilot whales, by the coastal drive fisheries, but they are no longer hunted here and are considered abundant.

Pacific White-sided Dolphin

Playful Pest

The Pacific white-sided dolphin is gregarious, sociable and high-spirited — reportedly even more so than its cousin, the Atlantic white-sided dolphin.

Gregarious: In a recent survey conducted by the Center for Coastal Marine Studies of the University of California, Santa Cruz, 46,000 Pacific white-sided dolphins were sighted in only 400 herds, an average of 115 animals per herd. Some herds numbered more than 1,000, and three herds topped 2,500.

Sociable: In nearly one-third of the sightings, Pacific white-sided dolphins were travelling and feeding with northern right whale dolphins and/or Risso's dolphins. Almost compulsively sociable, they are also observed with Dall's porpoises, humpback whales, sei whales, grey whales, blue whales, pilot whales and common dolphins, plus a wide variety of marine birds, seals, sea elephants and sea lions.

High-spirited: They surf, bow-ride and somersault in the best dolphin fashion, though their movements are difficult to measure. Once, an overenthusiastic Pacific white-sided dolphin at sea leapt 10 feet onto the deck of a moving research vessel. Their leaps in aquariums, where they have performed since the early 1960s, are higher and wilder than other captives. According to trainers, their antics reveal their greater curiosity as well as their mischievous nature, which rivals and sometimes exceeds that of captive bottlenose dolphins and killer whales. At the Vancouver Aquar-

PACIFIC WHITE-SIDED DOLPHIN

Lagenorhynchus obliquidens

ium, Whitewings — the Pacific white-sided dolphin sharing the tank with Hyak, the killer whale — has often stolen fish from the big male and playfully harassed him. At California's Marineland of the Pacific in the 1960s, a white-sided dolphin often pestered the slower-moving pilot whale until he was so upset, he would chase after the little dolphin, breaking all known pilot whale speed records.

Pacific white-sided dolphins are found well offshore in the North Pacific. In September and October, they form the largest herds, and sexual activity and juvenile antics seem to be the greatest then. They become less pelagic during the winter. By May, the herds are at their smallest — about 35 members on average.

BIOLOGICAL PROFILE

The **PACIFIC WHITE-SIDED DOLPHIN**, *Lagenorhynchus obliquidens*, is a toothed whale, Odontoceti, belonging to the family of oceanic dolphins called Delphinidae. It is sometimes called lag, white-striped dolphin or hook-finned porpoise.

Size

Pacific white-sided dolphins measure up to 7½ feet long and weigh at least 300 pounds. Calves are 2½ to 3 feet at birth.

Features

Pacific white-sided dolphins are somewhat robust with a short, thick beak, a sharply hooked dorsal fin and long, curved flippers. Both dorsal fin and flippers are slightly rounded at the tips. Colouring: black back,

flukes, beak, lips and around eyes, light grey sides, white belly and white or light grey "suspenders" along upper flanks; the forward part of the dorsal fin is dark, the rear part light; a narrow black stripe runs from corner of mouth to flipper. Pacific white-sided dolphins have 24 to 31 small, pointed teeth on each side of the lower jaw and 23 to 32 on each side of the upper jaw.

Diet

Pacific white-sided dolphins prey on squid, herring, sardines and anchovies and feed primarily at night. They sometimes smack the water with the head or tail when eating.

Natural History

Males and females reach sexual maturity when they are about 6 feet long. Calves are born in summer or early fall after a 10-to-12-month gestation. Year-round resident pods are found in some areas, such as off southern California. Pacific white-sided dolphins may form huge herds of more than 1,000, which contain animals of all ages and both sexes, but the average size is about 115 animals. They are highly social and are often seen travelling and feeding with other marine mammals. Pacific white-sided dolphins are acrobatic swimmers and will sometimes alternate riding a ship's bow wave and its wake. Some Pacific white-sided dolphins are killed accidentally in nets used by the salmon fisheries.

Range

Pacific white-sided dolphins like the temperate waters of the North Pacific. They are generally found well offshore along the B.C. coast.

Status

Pacific white-sided dolphins are one of the most abundant dolphins in the North Pacific.

Harbour Porpoise

The Puffing Pig

The lower Bay of Fundy, especially around the islands of southern New Brunswick, has one of the world's highest concentrations of harbour porpoises. Here, since the late 1960s, University of Guelph researchers led by David E. Gaskin have been investigating the species. From a variety of boats and shore lookouts, especially on Grand Manan Island, Gaskin has watched the herds arrive in the inshore areas every July.

Life for harbour porpoises during the summer seems to be centred on fishing. Their overall movement patterns closely resemble those of their main quarry — herring, mackerel and squid. The porpoises travel in very small, loose groups, some of which include a mature female and a calf.

As the summer progresses and the size of each herd increases — up to about 15 animals — they begin to move offshore, and by late October, most of the herds are gone. Gaskin and his colleagues have identified an inshore/offshore migratory pattern (rather than the north/south pattern usually found with whales), and they suspect that many of the porpoises head for Browns Bank and Georges Bank, south of Nova Scotia. Harbour porpoises seem to prefer the water temperatures there, which are about 45 to 48 degrees F, though a few — probably subadult males — overwinter in the much cooler waters of the Bay of Fundy.

The harbour porpoise is shy and wary of boats, and

HARBOUR PORPOISE

Phocoena phocoena

it is not a bow-rider. Yet because of its numbers, it is often observed passing boats in the Bay of Fundy, on the St. Lawrence and around Newfoundland. At about 5 feet and 100 pounds for an adult, the harbour porpoise is the smallest cetacean found in Canadian waters. A newborn calf is only 2 to 3 feet long. Harbour porpoises have a short life span, according to Gaskin — up to about 13 years, with an average of 8 to 9 years. And they have a surprisingly low reproductive rate. After maturity, cows give birth once a year at most, with some resting for 12 months or more between pregnancies. Although Gaskin and his colleagues have occasionally seen harbour porpoises mating in the inner island passage, most of the mating — and calving — seems to occur offshore.

Since harbour porpoises feed at the top of the food chain, they are probably a fairly good environmental indicator. In the tissues of harbour porpoises, Gaskin and his associates have found "DDT levels in excess of 500 ppm and polychlorinated biphenyls (PCBs) in excess of 200 ppm [both in blubber], together with significant quantities of HCBs and chlordanes. In the liver of this species, mercury levels of 90 ppm have been recorded in some specimens and, in a few animals, brain levels of about 8 ppm — close to those at which one might expect, on the basis of clinical studies of other mammals, that some symptoms of mercury poisoning might start to manifest themselves." The semiclosed circulation of the Bay of Fundy makes it susceptible to a buildup of contaminants. Industrial development must be kept to a minimum if whales, porpoises, fish and birds are to survive.

Harbour porpoises, once plentiful in the Baltic Sea and along the northern coast of Europe, have nearly disappeared today. Will Canadians let them disappear from Fundy?

BIOLOGICAL PROFILE

The **HARBOUR PORPOISE**, *Phocoena phocoena*, is a toothed whale, Odontoceti, belonging to the family of porpoises called Phocoenidae. In the

Maritimes, this porpoise is often called puffing pig; and in Quebec, *marsouin commun* or *pourcil*.

Size

Harbour porpoises are usually about 5 feet long and weigh approximately 100 pounds, although they may reach 6½ feet and 140 pounds. They are the smallest cetaceans found in Canadian waters. Calves are 2 to 3 feet at birth.

Features

Harbour porpoises are chunky, with tiny flippers and a triangular dorsal fin. They have a small rounded head with an indistinct beak and a short, straight mouth line that tilts slightly upward. Colouring: dark grey to black back, lighter below, often speckled in transition zone; greyish white area extends from belly up the sides in front of dorsal fin; grey line from mouth to flipper; some albinos have been reported. They have 19 to 28 small spade-shaped teeth on each side of both jaws.

Range

Harbour porpoises live in the coastal waters of the northern temperate and ice-free boreal zones, often in bays, harbours, estuaries and river mouths. They are widely distributed along both coasts of North America and are plentiful in the Bay of Fundy, the St. Lawrence River, the Gulf of St. Lawrence and around Newfoundland and Labrador. They are common along the West Coast from the Gulf of Alaska to California.

Diet

Harbour porpoises eat a variety of fish including small cod, herring, mackerel, pollack, sole and sardines, plus squid, octopus and crustaceans.

Status

Although the world population is unknown, their numbers are declining. Their near-shore range has made them vulnerable to environmental pollution and hunting, and many die when they become entangled in fishing nets. At least 4,000 are estimated to live in the lower Bay of Fundy and Passamaquoddy Bay.

Natural History

The reproductive cycle of the harbour porpoise has not been well defined, but it is thought that sexual maturity is reached at 4 to 6 years and that cows give birth every 1 to 2 years. They seem to have a very low reproductive rate. The mating season is probably from June through October. Most calves are born between May and July after an 11-month gestation. Nursing lasts 6 to 8 months. Their seasonal movements appear to be inshore-offshore, rather than north-south, and are probably dictated by food supplies and ice formation. Harbour porpoises are encountered singly, in pairs or in herds of 5 to 10, although groups of 50 or more have been observed. They are shy and difficult to approach. Harbour porpoises are active, but because they are wary of vessels, they do not ride bow waves. When on the move, they swim at speeds approaching 14 miles per hour and surface as many as 6 or 8 times at one-minute intervals. Other times, they swim slowly, quietly breaking at the surface. They are preyed upon by great white sharks and killer whales, and many die when they become trapped by fast-forming ice.

DALL'S PORPOISE

Phocoenoides dalli

Dall's Porpoise

Hyperactive Speed Demon

Few mammals on land or at sea are as active as the Dall's porpoise — certainly the fastest small cetacean. Reaching estimated speeds of 30 knots, travelling in groups of 2 to 10 or more, they shoot through the water, throwing up fancy splashes called rooster tails.

Dall's porpoises are unmistakably marked: Their bold black-and-white colour schemes suggest the drama of killer whales, but their lightning surfacing reveals only the all-black to all-white dorsal fins — and even they are a blur. Dalls whiz by — now zigzagging, now circling, now doing "crazy eights" — and are soon gone.

Once in a while, Dalls will ride the bow of a small boat or ship. The faster it's going, the better. Glimps-ing them then — all sleek and powerful and wagging their tail flukes up and down as they jet-propel themselves just beneath the water's surface — is exhilarating, but it is still just a fleeting glimpse. In many summers of meeting Dalls along the B.C. coast, I've seen them bow-ride only twice, and they are the only porpoise to do so. Far more common bow-riders are the three "lag" species of dolphins found off Canada — the Pacific white-sided dolphin off the west coast and the Atlantic white-sided and white-beaked dolphins off the east coast.

The only enemy of the Dall's porpoise is the killer whale — or so the records insist — but I have often watched killers and Dall's porpoises swimming side by side. They even share feeding areas, where the larder is apparently well stocked. The killer whales never seem aggressive, but the Dalls don't slow down enough to encourage the killers. I once watched six Dalls race into a killer whale pod. The whales were resting in circle formation, coming up slowly and dozing at the surface. But "surrounded," the Dalls were panic-stricken. For several minutes, they zigzagged back and forth across the circle as if trapped, then shot beneath the whales and were gone.

Any interest that killer whales might have in Dalls would likely be only seasonal. Most resident killer whales along the B.C. coast are confirmed fish-eaters. And although the rarely seen transient killer whales are marine-mammal eaters, they would have to work very hard to catch these speed demons. Perhaps a Dall's porpoise can't tell when a killer whale is hungry, but the sight or sound of orca seems enough to trigger the flight response, making the hyperactive porpoise even more hyperactive — they just can't seem to relax.

When cetacean authority Kenneth S. Norris was curator of California's Marineland of the Pacific in the 1950s, he tried to capture several Dall's porpoises for exhibit. All died quickly, beating their tails in a frenzy and battering their captors. Eventually, the United States Navy managed to keep one alive for a year and a half. Marty, as he was called, was responsive but nervous in training. To support his racing metabolic rate, he ate 28 to 30 pounds of fish a day — twice the amount a captive bottlenose dolphin consumes.

Dissecting Marty and other Dalls, United States Navy researcher Sam H. Ridgway found very thin blubber and a small brain compared with other dolphins he had studied. But each Dall's porpoise had a giant heart, giving the species one of the largest heart-to-body-weight ratios among all cetaceans.

BIOLOGICAL PROFILE

The **DALL'S PORPOISE**, *Phocoenoides dalli*, is a toothed whale, Odontoceti, belonging to the family of porpoises called Phocoenidae.

Size

Dall's porpoises measure up to more than 7 feet long and weigh up to 480 pounds. Calves are about a foot long at birth.

Features

Dall's porpoises are small but robust, with a tiny head, a steeply sloping forehead, a poorly defined beak, a narrow mouth and a protruding lower jaw. They have small, pointed flippers, a slightly curved to almost triangular dorsal fin, relatively broad flukes and a thick keel on the top and bottom of the tail stock. Colouring: shiny black, with large white flanks; dorsal fin often trimmed in white; lips and edge of tail flukes are occasionally white; some all-white, all-black and piebald individuals have been reported. Dall's porpoises have 19 to 28 teeth on each side of upper and lower jaws.

Diet

Dall's porpoises enjoy squid, crustaceans and schooling fish, such as capelin, mackerel, herring and anchovies.

Natural History

Females reach sexual maturity at 5½ feet, or almost 7 years, males at about 6 feet and 8 years. Cows probably give birth every 3 years after approximately an 11½-month gestation, and calves nurse about 2 years. In the western North Pacific, calving takes place mainly from July to September, but in the eastern North Pacific, the season is spread out over a longer period, with some births occurring year-round. Details of the movements of Dall's porpoises are poorly known. They usually travel in groups of 2 to 10, but up to 200 may gather on feeding grounds. Dall's porpoises are vigorous, fast swimmers. Their speedy surfacing throws up a rooster tail — a spray caused by the cone of water that comes off the head as it breaks the surface. Dall's porpoises have very jerky movements, darting swiftly about and often making steeply angled turns; but they rarely leap. They are capable of making deep dives. Dall's porpoises are preyed upon by killer whales.

Range

Dall's porpoises range throughout the North Pacific and may be found in sounds, inland passages, nearshore regions and the open sea. They are common off the B.C. coast, especially in the Inside Passage.

Status

Dall's porpoises are abundant throughout their range. Thousands were killed accidentally in the Japanese gill-net fishery for salmon off Alaska, but in recent years, this toll has decreased.

Further Reading

BROWER, K. 1979. *Wake of the Whale*. Friends of the Earth/Dutton, New York. 161 pp. Colour and black-and-white photographs by W. Curtsinger.

ELLIS, R. 1980. *The Book of Whales*. Alfred A. Knopf, New York. 252 pp. Colour illustrations.

ELLIS, R. 1982. *Dolphins and Porpoises*. Alfred A. Knopf, New York. 270 pp. Colour illustrations.

HALEY, D. (editor). 1978. *Marine Mammals of Eastern North Pacific and Arctic Waters*. Pacific Search Press, Seattle. 256 pp. Colour and black-and-white photographs.

HOYT, E. 1984. *Orca: The Whale Called Killer*. Camden House/Firefly, Toronto. 304 pp. Colour and black-and-white photographs.

HOYT, E. 1984. *The Whale Watcher's Handbook*. Penguin/Madison Press, Toronto. 208 pp. Black-and-white photographs; illustrations by Pieter A. Folkens.

KATONA, S.K., V. ROUGH AND D.T. RICHARDSON. 1983. *A Field Guide to the Whales, Porpoises and Seals of the Gulf of Maine and Eastern Canada: Cape Cod to Newfoundland*. Charles Scribner's Sons, New York. 256 pp. Black-and-white photographs and illustrations.

LEATHERWOOD, S., R.R. REEVES AND L. FOSTER. 1983. *The Sierra Club Handbook of Whales and Dolphins*. Sierra Club Books, San Francisco. 302 pp. Colour illustrations and black-and-white photographs.

MCNALLY, R. 1981. *So Remorseless A Havoc. Of Dolphins, Whales and Men*. Little, Brown and Co., Boston. 288 pp. Black-and-white photographs; illustrations by Pieter A. Folkens.

NORRIS, K.S. 1974. *The Porpoise Watcher: A naturalist's experiences with porpoises and whales*. W.W. Norton, New York. 250 pp. Black-and-white photographs.

PRYOR, K. 1975. *Lads Before the Wind: Adventures in porpoise training*. Harper & Row, New York. 278 pp. Black-and-white photographs.

SCAMMON, C.M. 1874. *The Marine Mammals of the North-Western Coast of North America, Described and Illustrated: Together With an Account of the American Whale-Fishery*. J.H. Carmany and Co., San Francisco. (Reprinted 1968 by Dover, New York.) 320 pp. Black-and-white illustrations.

Whale Research in Canada

The Atlantic

Department of Zoology
College of Biological Science
University of Guelph
Guelph, Ontario N1G 2W1

Ceta-Research Inc.
Box 10
Trinity, Newfoundland A0C 2S0

Whale Research Group
Memorial University of Newfoundland
St. John's, Newfoundland A1B 3X9

The Arctic

Arctic Biological Station**
Department of Fisheries and Oceans
555 St. Pierre Boulevard
St. Anne de Bellevue, Quebec H9X 3L6

World Wildlife Fund/Canada**
60 St. Clair Avenue East, Suite 201
Toronto, Ontario M4T 1N5

LGL Ltd.
44 Eglinton Avenue West
Toronto, Ontario M4R 1A1

The St. Lawrence

Mingan Island Cetacean Study
Box 159
Sept-Iles, Quebec G4R 4K3

The Pacific

West Coast Whale Research Foundation*
Box 49296
Four Bentall Centre
Vancouver, British Columbia V7X 1L3

Marine Mammal Research
Pacific Biological Station
Department of Fisheries and Oceans
Nanaimo, British Columbia V9R 5K6

Department of Zoology*
University of British Columbia
6270 University Boulevard
Vancouver, British Columbia V6T 1W5

Vancouver Aquarium*
Box 3232
Vancouver, British Columbia V6B 3X8

*Also involved in work in the Arctic
**Also involved in work in the St. Lawrence

John Oliphant

ERICH HOYT is the author of two recently published books on the subject of whales: *Orca: The Whale Called Killer* (Camden House) and *The Whale Watcher's Handbook* (Madison Press). He lives in Montreal and has written for many major publications, including *National Geographic*, *Oceans*, *Nature Canada* and *The New York Times*. Mr. Hoyt is a member of the Society for Marine Mammalogy and has spent thousands of hours watching and studying whales in Canadian waters. He writes frequently about marine mammals and other subjects in EQUINOX.